How to . . .

COLES NOTES

Key Point

Basic concepts in point form.

Close Up

Additional hints, notes, tips or background information.

Watch Out!

Areas where problems frequently occur.

Quick Tip

Concise ideas to help you learn what you need to know.

Remember This!

Essential material for mastery of the topic.

COLES NOTES

Your Guide to . . .

Dogs & Dog Care

Choosing the right breed

Training your dog

Care, feeding & health

COLES NOTES have been an indispensable aid to students on five continents since 1948.

COLES NOTES now offer titles on a wide range of general interest topics as well as traditional academic subject areas and individual literary works. All COLES NOTES are written by experts in their fields and reviewed for accuracy by independent authorities and the Coles Editorial Board.

COLES NOTES provide clear, concise explanations of their subject areas. Proper use of COLES NOTES will result in a broader understanding of the topic being studied. For academic subjects, COLES NOTES are an invaluable aid for study, review and exam preparation. For literary works, COLES NOTES provide interesting interpretations and evaluations which supplement the text but are not intended as a substitute for reading the text itself. Use of the NOTES will serve not only to clarify the material being studied, but should enhance the reader's enjoyment of the topic.

COLES PUBLISHING. A division of Prospero Books
Toronto - Canada
Printed in Canada

Cataloguing in Publication Data
Bogart, Jo Ellen, 1945-

Your guide to ... dogs and dog care : choosing the right breed, care, feeding & health, training your dog

(Coles notes) ISBN 0-7740-0591-2

1. Dogs. I. Title. II. Series

SF426.B64 1999 636.7'0887 C99-931035-6

Publisher: Nigel Berrisford
Editing: Paul Kropp Communications
Book design and layout: Karen Petherick, Markham, Ontario
Illustration: Kristen Nakamura

Manufactured by Webcom Limited
Cover finish: Webcom's Exclusive DURACOAT

Contents

CHAPTER ONE

Deciding to get a dog

WHAT IS INVOLVED IN DOG OWNERSHIP?

If you are thinking of getting a dog, there are many aspects to consider. Getting a dog means, or *should* mean, taking on a long-term commitment. The main idea of dog ownership is sharing, since you will be sharing your time, space and resources with your dog. Are you the kind of person who is willing to do this?

Dogs are social animals; they crave interaction. They want to be with you, see you, hear your voice and look to you for leadership. Some dogs will be happy to share your couch-potato hours snoozing at your feet or sharing the sofa, but others will want active games or even intellectual stimulation. Also, dogtime does not always follow a human schedule, for instance, when the pooch gets into something that makes a bath immediately necessary. Does your time schedule lend itself to such an investment of time? Such flexibility?

What about space? Dogs actually take up space with their bodies and their stuff. Like kids, dogs require certain pieces of equipment: beds, crates, toys, leashes, feeding dishes, food. A dog might be underfoot at times, even if well trained. Again, sharing is the key word.

There are many expenses involved in owning a dog, ranging from hundreds to over a thousand dollars a year. Good-quality food is not cheap and routine medical care will run over $100 a year. There is also the chance of non-routine medical care in case of illness or accident. As well as the dog-care essentials, there are many tempting pet toys and supplies that you might find irresistible. Many areas require licensing of dogs. It is also possible that expensive changes to your home, such as fencing the yard, might be necessary. There might even be some damage caused by the dog, especially in the chewing-puppy stage. If you are not prepared to take on training the dog yourself, there is the cost of a training course.

Dogs, while intelligent creatures, need supervision and care to remain safe and healthy. Dogs tend to follow their own interests, somewhat like children, with little regard for the dangers that are present in the world today. As an owner, you must protect your dog from disease, traffic and other hazards. As well, you must make sure that other people are protected from bad behavior on the part of your dog. You should make sure your pet does not breed indiscriminately, and probably not at all. You must be prepared to stoop and scoop and you must provide for your pet's care if you must be away.

Dogs can be messy. Through no fault of the dog's, its hair will find its way into every part of your house. Brushing will help, but will not eliminate the problem. Brushing and other types of grooming will take your time, or your money to pay someone else to do it. Some breeds require the expense of regular clipping for their constantly growing coats. If you have allergies or are extremely picky about the state of your home, you might not be a good prospective dog owner.

Of course, some of these factors that seem like disadvantages might actually be advantages. Sharing your time and space can be beneficial. Some people find having another living creature in the house to be wonderfully comforting and satisfying. They come to love the sound of footsteps, the warm greetings and another living presence. A gentle nudge from a dog might be just what you need to get you out of the computer chair for some fresh air and exercise. A happy doggy smile and wagging tail might inject some humor and joy into your life. If you are called on to be more patient or more compassionate because of your connection to your pet, that just might be a good thing, too.

DOGS AND THE LAW

Your community probably requires your dog to be licensed. A license makes it easier to return your dog to you if it gets lost.

The funds raised with license fees often go, at least in part, to the local humane society or agency in charge of picking up and housing loose dogs. A responsible community will require at least a rabies vaccination as a prerequisite for licensing. There are probably also laws requiring your dog to be on leash when not otherwise under control, such as behind a fence, and laws requiring owners to clean up after their dogs. There are also anti-cruelty laws intended to protect animals from mistreatment and laws limiting the number of animals that can be legally housed in one dwelling.

Tort law deals with liability of an owner for his or her dog's behavior. You will usually be held responsible for injuries or damage to property brought about by your dog. Your insurance agent can tell you about liability insurance for dog damage.

Does dog ownership seem like a big deal? It is. But you don't have to decide quickly ... read on. The more you know, the more prepared you are to make the right decision. Dogs have been bred into so many forms that there might be a dog just right for you.

WHAT KIND OF DOG IS RIGHT FOR YOU?

While you are considering your appropriateness as a dog owner, you are also uncovering information that will help you decide on the kind of dog that would suit you best. Dogs come in a variety of sizes, activity levels, coat lengths, personalities and levels of instructability. Of course, it is necessary to remember that breed characteristics are not at all clear-cut. Dogs, like people, are affected both by their genetic makeup and by life experiences, so a dog is always a package of potential that you can work with to create a wonderful pet. Breed descriptions are only an indication of averages, never a guarantee of any given characteristic. Nevertheless, it is a good idea to pay attention to the descriptions because they give you some idea of what to expect.

So, what are the characteristics of you and your lifestyle that might influence your choice of a dog companion? How much space, interior and exterior, do you have to share with a dog? Small dogs simply take up less space and can sometimes get enough exercise simply by running around inside. Surprisingly, some large breeds seem content to lie around quietly while inside, as long as they get some active time outside. Another consideration is the closeness of neighbors, since some types of dogs tend to bark more than others.

How active are you? Will you want to share outdoor activities such as walking, hiking, jogging, swimming? Larger dogs have the strength and stamina to share really active sports. A tiny dog or one with very short legs will not be able to gallop along beside a jogger or cross-country skier. Some water-loving dogs, being good swimmers with suitable coats, will readily share water activities with their owners. If you travel a lot, smaller dogs fit in the car and in motel rooms more easily. Big dogs can usually stand the cold better, as can dogs with denser coats. Snub-nosed dogs are more prone to heat-related problems.

How involved do you want to be? Though all dogs need and enjoy some human interaction, some breeds seem to be more independent than others.

Who else shares your living space? If there are children, you will want to choose a breed that is known to get along well with children, patiently tolerating the less-than-perfect handling that children might give. Some nervous breeds are just too snappy for kids and some small breeds are too delicate. Starting with a dog older than a puppy might be advisable. Will there be other pets in the house? Some dogs such as terriers, bred to hunt vermin, might be nerve-wracking company for small furry pets, while other dogs, such as the herders, have a more benign or protective attitude toward other animals.

If you are not an experienced dog owner, you will want to avoid dogs with dominant personalities that require strict training. Dogs bred to guard aggressively fall into this category. Large powerful dogs, especially, should be avoided by those not willing to put a lot of patient and skilled work into a dog's training. Many dogs have ended up in shelters or put down because inexperienced, careless owners did not give them the training they needed.

Are you a gardener or very fussy about your yard? Some dogs, such as terriers, have a real fondness for digging. Selective fencing can help with this problem, as can choosing a breed not so prone to digging.

A full encyclopedia of dog breeds will give very explicit descriptions of breed characteristics, personalities and needs and is a fascinating read. Characteristics of dogs of mixed parentage are harder to predict, but vets and shelter workers can sometimes supply information that might be helpful.

Think about yourself:

- How much time do you have for a dog?
- Do you stay home or travel?
- How neat do you like your house?
- Do you have children? Other pets?
- How big is your house and yard?

Think about your potential dog:

- Large, small, medium sized?
- Active or easygoing?
- Long or short hair?
- Personality type?

WHERE TO GET YOUR DOG

This is a more complicated question than you might imagine. If you had a dog when you were a kid, it might have just wandered up to the house and stayed, or it might have been offspring from your aunt's dog who had pups. Times were simpler some years ago, before dogs - especially purebred dogs - became big business.

If you are thinking of getting a purebred dog, you would not want to support the sort of breeders who breed for profit only, without regard to the health and quality of the pups produced. Such establishments have come to be called "puppy mills" and often provide only squalid living conditions, poor food and no medical attention. Pups produced in such deplorable conditions sometimes end up at puppy wholesalers or pet stores. Such puppies can have serious health problems and will surely not have been socialized to be good companions. Most large-scale commercial breeders have better conditions than those just described, but you are much better off with the reputable breeder who takes every precaution with each litter and is an expert on her breed.

If you decide to get a purebred dog, you have several options. The first is the reputable breeder whose aim is the improvement of the breed. She will match the sire (father) and the dam (mother) in such a way as to optimize desirable characteristics. She will study bloodlines carefully and will often send her female away to be bred with a good match, rather than always breed from her own dogs. She will also make sure that all breeding stock is certified free of genetic defects known to the breed, if such testing is possible. She will be able to show certificates affirming the disease-free status of both parents. This breeder will not overlook the importance of temperament when choosing which dogs to breed.

What purebread means

Remember that the purebred certification is not a warranty of quality or dog personality, it only certifies parentage. A good breeder is your best assurance of a good dog.

The responsible breeder will ask you questions to make sure you will be a caring owner for her puppy. She will be able and willing to give advice on all aspects of dog care and will be willing to take the pup back if things do not work out. She will also be willing to show you the kennels where the dogs live and to let you meet the mother. The responsible breeder will not have so many litters that she is too busy to socialize the puppies. Nor will she be working with many breeds since it is important that she be well informed about the breed in which she specializes. She will be willing to spend the money to get the best veterinary care for all of her dogs. She will supply all registration paperwork pertaining to the purebred status of the dog free of charge.

Once you choose several breeds that seem to match your situation, you will want to study them carefully. Visiting a dog show is an excellent way to see the dogs and perhaps have the chance to talk to some breeders.

Other sources of purebred dogs are the local shelter or the rescue societies associated with various breeds. For more information regarding these sources, see the chapter on adopting the second-hand dog.

WHERE TO GET A MIXED-BREED DOG

Perhaps a purebred dog is not your choice. Dogs of mixed parentage can be excellent pets. Though they are not free of the genetic problems that have come to plague some purebreds in recent years, the incidence of this is probably lower.

There are several sources of mixed-breed dogs. Sometimes it is possible to get a puppy from a friend or acquaintance whose dog has had a litter. Some people feel that a responsible pet owner would have had the pet neutered and the pregnancy would never have happened. There is some truth to this. However, if the owner of the parent dog is someone you know to provide good quality food, vet care and a friendly home environment - and the parent dog is of good temperament - this source of a mixed-breed dog might work out all right. The two advantages of getting a puppy from a friend are that you know the birth circumstances and that *you* will be providing the early upbringing.

Mixed-breed dogs are highly unpredictable as to size and other characteristics. A real advantage to adopting an older dog is that it will be closer to its final size, might show more of its true personality and will probably be house-trained. While some dogs will have been damaged in various ways by abandonment or poor care, there are many fine dogs in shelters deserving of your love and care, and eager to be your devoted companion.

Where to find your dog?

Professional breeder	Expensive	Best for purebred and pedigreed dogs; a good breeder provides advice and ensures good early training and care
Part-time breeder	Varies	Sometimes an excellent source for purebred dogs; sometimes not
Newspaper ad	Varies	Investigate carefully before you buy
Pet store	Expensive	Care can be good or poor; some pet stores provide papers, some don't; most look after first shots
Friend or neighbor	Cheap	Workable for a mixed-breed dog if you feel the care was adequate and parent dog good-natured; perhaps no shots
Shelter	Cheap	Dog background is often unknown; preliminary shots are taken care of

CHAPTER TWO

Popular breeds

For full descriptions of the breeds recognized by each kennel club, you can consult the official kennel club books, available at your local library. Here is a sampling of some popular breeds, arranged by American Kennel Club groups.

SPORTING GROUP

An alert and energetic group that includes many hunting dogs. They are known for stamina as well as agility. Included are Pointers, Setters, Retrievers, Spaniels and more. Trainability varies.

Golden Retriever

This attractive and sturdy dog of 25-35 kg (60-75 lb.), was originally developed in England to recover birds for hunters. Today the breed has several lines to serve the various roles it plays, including gundog, field trial dog, helper dog for people with disabilities and dog for showing or family companion. It is generally very mild-mannered and good with children. Grooming needs are relatively light and the dog adapts well to urban living. Because of its size and natural exuberance, the Golden Retriever needs training to contain its impulse to be overly friendly.

Labrador Retriever

Perhaps the most popular dog in North America, the Labrador Retriever, called a Lab for short, was developed in Newfoundland. It was called the Labrador when it got to England, perhaps to keep from confusing it with the big black Newfoundland dog. In England it helped fishermen retrieve nets and also brought back waterfowl for hunters. The large 25-35 kg (60-75 lb.), powerful dog has a short coat that repels water and a heavy tapering tail like an otter. The handsome Lab comes in three coat colors: black, yellow and chocolate brown. The Lab's keen sense of smell helps with hunting and drug detection work.

These patient and intelligent dogs also serve as guide dogs for the blind. Labs make fine family dogs. They are exuberantly playful and take training very well. The short, hard coat sheds quite a bit so frequent brushing is recommended. Regular exercise suits this active dog, but the Lab can also be quiet in the house.

American Cocker Spaniel

This breed originated in Spain, but many types of Spaniel were developed in England where they were used to hunt woodcocks. Cockers today are bred for show and as companions. The American Cocker Spaniel came from the Cockers brought from England, but developed its own characteristics and was given breed status in 1947 in the United States when the original type came to be called the English Cocker Spaniel. The American Cocker Spaniel has a shorter back, a sloping backline, shorter muzzle and more domed skull than its English cousins. For many years the Cocker was the most popular dog in the United States. When well-bred, the Cocker is a trustworthy, easily trained pet. The popularity it has enjoyed has brought about some indiscriminate breeding and behavior problems, so choose a breeder carefully.

HOUND GROUP

Includes scent hounds that hunt by smell and sighthounds that hunt by sight. The dogs range in size from the miniature Dachshund to the towering Irish Wolfhound.

Beagle

A little hound with a big voice is the Beagle, a breed that originated in Great Britain and was useful for its rabbit-hunting skills. The 8-14 kg (18-30 lb.) dog resembles the larger Foxhound. Some Beagles in the past have been small enough to fit in the saddlebags of hunters. Beagles, like most hounds, are independent and somewhat headstrong. They typically hunt in packs and are, therefore, quite sociable. Beagle owners should be prepared to provide a lot of stimulation and companionship.

Besides a strong need for activity, the Beagle likes to wander and will dig out of a fence that is not secure. Chasing a scent is the Beagle's life and it will just keep going and going. Don't take your Beagle out without a leash. The Beagle's bay can be very annoying to neighbors, so don't leave a Beagle at home all day while you work. Beagles are bred in two sizes, 33 and 38 cm (13 and 15 in.), and in two types. The type bred for field trials is more packoriented and active, thus less adaptable to a single-dog home environment. The type bred for show is smaller and has a temperament more suited to life with a family. Grooming includes regular brushing and ear hygiene.

Basset Hound

The Basset Hound gets its name from the French word *bas*, which means low. This low-slung dog originated in France in the 1500s and was brought to the North American colonies by the English and the French. The Basset has a sense of smell second only to its ancestor, the Bloodhound, and is easy to follow in the field because of its pace and a tail that is held high. The long ears, wrinkles and fleshy droopy lips all help gather the scent. The long, large body of the Basset makes it a heavy dog at 18-36 kg (40-80 lb.), though it is only 35 cm (14 in.) at the shoulder.

The Basset Hound adapts well to urban living, with adequate exercise, and gets along with other animals as well as children. It is an affectionate and devoted pet. The long ears create a humid environment that must be kept cleaned out to avoid trouble. Aside from the ears, grooming is minimal. Use of a narrow food and water bowl is a good idea. Bassets can suffer from back problems worsened by weight gain. They are prone to gastric torsion, so two smaller meals a day is the rule. The feature of the Basset that bothers some owners the most is the unavoidable drool.

Borzoi

While the Basset Hound and the Beagle are scent hounds, the Borzoi hunts by sight and is called a sighthound or gazehound. This large 35-48 kg (75-105 lb.) and elegant dog was originally bred to hunt wolves, thus its earlier name, Russian Wolfhound. Unlike another sighthound, the smooth-coated Greyhound, the Borzoi has a warm coat suitable for a cold climate. The breed has a very deep chest and long legs with bones that are blade-shaped, rather than round, for better aerodynamics. Borzois are slow to mature; males are often not neutered until 18 months so that they can have time to develop the characteristic build of the breed. Calm, with a sweet personality, the Borzoi is good with children if raised with them and they do not tease or startle. Prospective owners need to know that Borzois like to chase small animals including cats, rabbits and even small dogs in the family. They do seem to really enjoy the company of other sighthounds. This dog needs space to run and will not develop properly without it. The legs are subject to fracture and the coat needs frequent brushing. Borzoi owners need to guard against bloat.

HERDING GROUP

Added to the AKC roster in 1983, this group includes breeds previously included in the working group. All are attuned to the movements of other animals and were originally developed to herd livestock.

German Shepherd

The German Shepherd (known in serious dog circles as the German Shepherd Dog) is a large dog, ranging from 34-43 kg (75-95 lb.). The breed can have many beautiful coat types including the commonly seen black and tan short-haired coat, the long black, the long sable, the long cream and the short white. The German Shepherd was bred for work and takes training well, though it requires a firm hand and an experienced dog owner to train successfully. Originally a sheep herder, the German Shepherd has moved into many areas of work, most notably as police and armed services dogs, rescue dogs and guide dogs for the blind. The breed came into being through the work of a German cavalry officer in the 1890s and today the breed is one of the most popular in the world. This popularity has caused some indiscriminate breeding and problems with temperament as well as physical health. A carefully bred German Shepherd is reliable, calm and obedient. It is naturally aloof, but can be very loyal to its family. The breed thrives on exercise and companionship. Like the Lab, the German Shepherd sheds a lot and needs brushing.

Collie

Rough Collie

Smooth Collie

Another working dog is the well-known Collie. This intelligent herding dog comes in two coat lengths. The coat of the Rough Collie, long and luxuriant, is familiar from the famous TV and cinema Collie, Lassie, and was originally the perfect raincoat for an outdoors dog. The less common Smooth Collie is essentially the same dog without the long hair (indeed, both the rough and the smooth have been found in the same litter). The smooth was used to drive sheep to market and its short coat prevented overheating. The breed was developed in Scotland and the Collie was a popular dog at shows in America by the 1880s. Though now a large dog, some 60 cm (24 in.) at the shoulder and 23-30 kg (50-65 lb.), the earlier dogs were smaller. The Collie, like all herding dogs, is intelligent and responsive to commands, but also capable of independent functioning. It takes well to training, but needs mental stimulation and exercise. It can be a barker. The rough coat requires considerable work to keep looking attractive. While many Collies are wonderful with children, indiscriminate breeding has produced some high-strung, nervous dogs.

WORKING GROUP

Dogs bred for tasks such as pulling carts, guarding homes and property, pulling sleds and performing rescue are included in the working group. This group includes the Siberian Husky, the Newfoundland, the Rottweiler, the Great Dane and more large, powerful dogs, as well as some smaller breeds such as the tiny tailless barge dog, the Schipperke. Their size and strength makes some of these breeds unsuitable for the average family. Others of the group, however, adapt well to urban family life.

Boxer

The Boxer is one of many breeds to originate in Germany about a hundred years ago. Its ancestors might have included fighting dogs of Tibet, the Mastiff and, more recently, the Bulldog. The name seems to refer to the dog's practice of fighting or playing with its front paws up. The Boxer was once used for fighting, but has also been used for police work. This square-headed, well-muscled dog is a fun-loving family pet that keeps its puppy attitude, but is gentle with children. The sleek, short coat is easy to care for, but does not give much protection from the cold. The boxer weighs in at 27-32 kg. (60-70 lb.), but moves with agility. It needs firm but gentle handling as it is somewhat sensitive. Boxers are loyal and protective toward family and wary of strangers, but self-confident. The shape of the Boxer muzzle causes the breed some breathing difficulties such as wheezing and snorting and makes it less comfortable in hot weather.

Great Dane

This giant breed, the national dog of Germany, was probably developed by mixing Greyhounds with Mastiffs in the Middle Ages. The Dane's great size 46-54 kg (100-120 lb.) and long easy stride allowed it to excel in the boar hunting for which it was used. Great Dane coat colors include fawn, black, blue, brindle and a harlequin made up of white with black patches. The once-cropped ears are often left untouched, giving the dog a gentle expression to match its easy-going personality. The Great Dane is a fine family pet, tolerant of children and easy to groom, but needs attention to be happy, and costs a lot to feed.

TERRIER GROUP

This group includes many breeds of feisty and energetic dogs, bred to kill vermin, that retain their pugnaciousness toward other animals. This groups includes the large Airedale and American Staffordshire Terrier and the very popular Miniature Schnauzer. The smaller terriers are very active and inclined to take charge.

Norfolk Terrier and Norwich Terrier

Norfolk Terrier

These two breeds are almost identical, having been, at one time, the same breed. The ears are the main difference, the Norfolk having drop ears, the Norwich having prick (stand-up) ears. Developed in Great Britain in the 1800s for rat hunting, they are about 25 cm (10 in.) at the shoulder and weigh in at about 5-5 1/2 kg (12 lb.). They are excellent companions and watchdogs, alert, happy and fearless. The small size makes them easy to exercise in confined spaces. They both come in tones of red, golden, black and tan and a lighter whitish color. The coat requires little work to groom, but gives protection from cooler weather.

Norwich Terrier

These dogs get along well with children, but might pester a cat if it is not introduced carefully, and will be dangerous, obviously, for pet rodents. They are a basically healthy little breed, though their teeth are prone to crowding and might need extra dental care. They do like to dig and bark. Though they love their owners, they are not to be trusted off leash as they will run off.

TOY GROUP

Made up of small breeds, though small breeds are included in almost every group. These dogs are a good size for apartments and don't eat, shed or poop as much as their bigger relatives. These lapdogs are lovable and loyal and some can travel in the airplane cabin with you. They're also smart.

Chihuahua

Chihuahua

Long-haired Chihauhua

This tiny dog is just 13 cm (5 in.) at the shoulder and weighs 2.7 kg (6 lb.), perfect for apartment living. The breed is said to have originated in Mexico from ancestors that lived with the Toltecs and later the Maya. It was developed further in the United States, and crosses with other breeds brought about a long-haired variety. Today the breed comes in many lovely colors, solid and mixed, in both long hair and short. This dog can be jealous of other pets and can also be a little snappish at times if it feels insecure. It often bonds strongly with one person and is especially good for older people. The Chihuahua seems to like members of its own breed best. It is fine with children who are careful not to be rough, but the dog is not always easy to housebreak. As with many small dogs, the Chihuahua is long-lived and is susceptible to tooth problems. Feed this dog crunchy food some of the time to help prevent plaque. If you choose to get a Chihuahua, don't go for the smallest, as it is likely to be frail.

NON-SPORTING GROUP

A diverse group made up of dogs that don't fit in other groups. This group includes the very popular Poodle and Lhasa Apso, the sporty Dalmatian and some lesser-known pooches.

Dalmatian

The Dalmatian has a long history, being known in Dalmatia, which is now a part of Croatia, perhaps having been taken there from India. The spotted dog appeared in very early art work and accompanied gypsies and their caravans. Classified today as a non-sporting dog, the breed has been used for many tasks including wardog, sentinel, herder, retriever, performer and draft dog. However, the job for which it is best known, and for which it is bred, is to run with horses as a carriage dog. The Dalmatian gets along well with horses, keeping them in line and clearing the way for the coach. The dog has become well known for working with firefighters and riding on the fire wagon.

The medium-sized dog of 23–25 kg (50–55 lb.) is born white, but develops the characteristic black spots before long.

The lovely coat sheds a lot, but daily brushing will help. Because it was bred to run long distances, this dog needs lots of exercise and can become destructive and neurotic if it does not get it. The Dalmatian is unique among dogs in that it can suffer from bladder stones, which can be expensive to treat. It is also susceptible to deafness. This highly energetic dog can cause problems for the quiet, inactive family and is not the dog for the inexperienced. In recent years, the Dalmatian has gained fame as Sparky the fire prevention mascot and in the Disney movie *101 Dalmatians*. As is often the case with increased popularity, there has been careless, profit-motivated breeding and uninformed or impulse buying. For these reasons, there are many homeless Dalmatians in shelters.

Poodle

Miniature Poodle

The Poodle comes in three convenient sizes: standard, miniature and toy. The large Poodles were the originators of the breed and were water-loving gundogs. The lion-like haircut that is still popular for show dogs was designed to help the dogs swim better while offering some protection from the cold water. The breed's fine sense of smell made Poodles excellent truffle-finding dogs and their trainability made them fine circus performers. The Poodle's coat is wiry, curly, woolly and warm. It can be cut in many styles, but if left uncut will mat into long cords such are seen in the Corded Poodle. The Poodle coat is said to be less allergenic than other dogs' coats, but it does require continual grooming to keep it in decent shape. Most pet Poodles wear the sporting clip, which is about an inch long all over.

All Poodles are intelligent dogs, but the standards are more docile and stable. The smaller poodles might be more demanding of attention and a bit yappy. All make entertaining pets.

Lhasa Apso

This small 6-7 kg (13-15 lb.) breed originated in Tibet where its name meant "Bark Lion Sentinel Dog." Its keen hearing and intelligence made it well adapted for its job as indoor watch-dog in palaces. The Lhasa arrived in the West in 1921 and by 1934 had been distinguished from the Chinese breed, the *Shih Tzu*, with which it shares some ancestry. The Lhasa has since become a very popular breed. Its long, straight, coarse coat comes in a number of shades, often multicolored, and of course, needs a lot of grooming. As with many small dogs, it has a long lifespan of 13-14 years.

The most popular breeds

1. Labrador Retriever	Large, friendly, responsive, water-loving; can get fat
2. Rottweiler	Large, protective; popularity and mishandling have led to aggressive behavior in some cases
3. German Shepherd	Large, popular worldwide, versatile, intelligent, but can have poor tempers
4. Golden Retriever	Large, responsive, good with children,
5. Beagle	Medium-sized, affectionate, friendly and lively; can wander
6. Poodle	Three sizes, all intelligent, pleasant companions; much grooming required
7. Dachshund	Small, short-legged hound in two sizes and three coat types; hardy and vigorous, good house companion and watchdog
8. Cocker Spaniel	Once a bird-hunting dog, now a responsive, affectionate medium-sized companion; many coat shades, needs much grooming
9. Yorkshire Terrier	Tiny breed with a very long silky coat; world's most popular Terrier; tenacious, stubborn and energetic
10. Pomeranian	Toy spitz-type dog, good watch dog, good companion; needs a lot of grooming
11. Shih Tzu	Small, cold-tolerant, playful, good with other dogs and kids; needs lots of grooming
12. Chihuahua	World's smallest breed; fragile, gets cold easily, needs little grooming, good companion, long-lived
13. Boxer	Large, playful, affectionate, active, feisty with children, responsive, sensitive to cold

continued ...

The most popular breeds

14.	Shetland Sheepdog	A miniature of the Rough Collie; has herding instinct, takes instruction well, wary of strangers, good with children
15.	Dalmatian	Large, exuberant, needs room to run, little grooming required
16.	Miniature Schnauzer	Small, good companion, trainable, good watchdog, good city dweller; needs frequent grooming
17.	Siberian Husky	Medium to large, strong and athletic, cold-tolerant, good companion; needs room to run
18.	Miniature Pinscher	Small, feisty German-bred Terrier, good jumper, can be snappy, short no-groom coat, good watchdog
19.	Pug	Small, short-haired, flat-faced, and long-lived; stubborn and strong-willed, but affectionate; sheds year-round
20.	Doberman Pinscher	Large, well-muscled, powerful, alert and obedient; needs careful training and good socialization; choose from good temperament line; little grooming required.
21.	Boston Terrier	Small, short-haired, good temperament, long-lived; suitable for urban living
22.	Basset Hound	Long and heavy, gentle, good with children; tolerant of wide range of temperatures
23.	Maltese	Small with long, silky white hair that needs daily grooming; good-tempered with children, lively and intelligent
24.	German Short-haired Pointer	Large, short-haired, sporty and athletic; good companion for the city or the country; long-lived

The most popular breeds

25.	English Springer Spaniel	Medium-sized, long-haired hunting dog that needs mental and physical stimulation to avoid destructive behavior; choose carefully for temperament; moderate grooming
26.	Chow Chow	Large, full-coated, powerful dog; not recommended for families with children; snappy tendencies; a one-person dog.
27.	Bulldog	Medium-sized, muscular and powerful, with a huge head; health problems can result from extreme body form; gentle and entertaining companion
28.	Pekinese	Small, short-legged, flat-faced, stubborn; good with children; needs frequent grooming
29.	Rough Collie	Large, long-haired, trainable, good with children; good watchdog; needs daily grooming
30.	Bichon Frise	Small, white and fluffy; needs lots of grooming of coat and teeth; responsive, vivacious and affectionate

CHAPTER THREE

Adopting a second-hand dog

WHY ARE THERE SO MANY HOMELESS DOGS?

In a nation with many dog lovers, there are, nevertheless, many more dogs than there are good homes available for them. Local shelters are full of dogs suitable for adoption into good homes, but many of these will never be adopted. There are many reasons for this sad situation. Some people fail to neuter their pets, allowing them to breed indiscriminately, whereas the truly responsible breeder will have homes lined up for his pups before breeding his female. Sometimes dog owners suffer changes in circumstances beyond their control and feel that they simply cannot take care of the dog they already have. Others choose a dog that does not properly suit their needs, and when the going gets rough they surrender the dog to a shelter in hopes that it might find a more suitable owner.

What will you find at a shelter? Shelters typically have dogs of all descriptions, from the very young to the middle aged. Older dogs are often judged to be less desirable and are put to sleep. This is unfortunate, because many older dogs still have lots of good years in them and make fine and devoted pets. Smaller dogs often live active lives well into their teen years, so a seven-year-old is only middle-aged. Many dogs will be of mixed parentage, but there will often be purebreds too. There are often many dogs of a breed that has become fashionable and which people buy without thorough investigation.

You might wonder why people would buy a purebred dog and then turn it in to a shelter. What are the reasons for any dog to be turned in? The stated reasons might be destructiveness or difficulty in housebreaking, nippiness with kids or the dog needing more room to run, but the underlying reasons might stack up more like:

- Poor choice of dog for the person in the first place. The owner didn't educate himself adequately before choosing a dog and got an unsuitable one.
- Poor training. The owner didn't get right in there with the necessary structure and routine for the dog in the beginning and poor behavior was the result.
- Poor dedication on the part of the owner to get through the difficult adolescent period. Sometimes a failure to spay or neuter contributes to this problem.

Two good places to find second-hand dogs are shelters or humane societies and breed-rescue societies. If you are thinking of getting a dog from a shelter, there are some things you can do to increase your chances of getting a dog that fits you and your lifestyle. Visit the shelter several times to get a feel for the place. Talk to the workers about the dogs. Read the histories of the dogs to see where they have come from and what they might have experienced. If you take the dogs, one at a time, to a holding or visitation area, or out for a walk, you can start to see which ones relate best to you. Try not to feel guilty for refusing a dog if it is not right for you. The dog that is not right for you might be just right for someone else.

The dogs being offered for adoption by breed-rescue societies will typically be dogs of one specific breed. Some rescue societies will take information from you as the prospective owner of a rescued dog. They will then match you with the animal they feel is best suited to you, or suggest several to consider. While shelters have dogs of all descriptions in one location, breed-rescue groups place rescued dogs in foster homes with people interested in the breed. The foster owners will be able to describe in detail the temperament of the dog and probably its history, as well as give some advice on the characteristics of the breed. Sometimes dogs from rescue societies will be located far from where you live, so transportation will have to be arranged. However, a careful search can often turn up some fine candidates for adoption closer to home.

There are other opportunities to adopt second-hand dogs. Vets sometimes know of dogs in need of a new home and can help with adoptions. Sometimes private adoptions take place when you just happen to hear of someone who must give up a dog. Ads in the paper can sometimes lead to successful adoptions. However, in these cases, it is good to ask a lot of questions of the person giving up the dog. Especially ask which veterinarian has been seeing the dog regularly. A vet checkup before final arrangements is a good idea, as well. You want to know of any serious health problems before committing to a new pet.

There is another source of previously owned dogs that might not come to mind. Organizations that train dogs for special purposes such as leading the blind, or aiding the physically impaired, train to a very high standard. Dogs that fail to make the grade are sometimes available for adoption by people who do not need the special services for which the dogs were trained. For people who do have special needs, dogs are made available at a fraction of the substantial cost of training them. Organizations that train dogs for the deaf sometimes recruit new dog trainees at shelters. Retired guide dogs for the blind are sometimes adopted after their years of service are over.

WHAT TO EXPECT OF THE SECOND-HAND DOG

Any dog undergoing a change of owner will be in an unsettled position and have special needs. The well-loved dog that was bonded to a previous owner will be missing that person badly and will be confused about what has happened to that person. This dog will be mourning the loss of a relationship.

The dog that has grown up in the streets will have a different set of problems. Many of the skills that kept the street dog alive will not endear it to people. Used to foraging for food wherever he can find it, he might take food left within reach. The dog that has never had a home will be unaccustomed to the common noises of a household and will find them unsettling. This dog will have no manners, though with patience, you can teach him to behave.

The dog that has had a home, but has been poorly treated,

will have formed his ideas about people from the bad experiences he has had in the past. He might be overly aggressive or cowering and submissive. He might show both kinds of behavior at different times. Any dog going through the stress of getting used to a new situation needs and deserves patience, security and understanding. The changes that take place in the dog as it settles in might not be rapid and might not be complete for quite a while. Habits you thought had been corrected might pop up again in times of stress. You might never know or understand some of the strange phobias and behaviors your dog is showing, but you can help your new pet overcome most of them and perhaps you can learn to live with the rest.

Your second-hand dog, faced with new people and surroundings, will have a great opportunity to learn. It is not just young dogs that are able to adapt to change. One of the best gifts you can give your adopted dog is the security of rules. If the rules stay the same, your dog can come to rely on what reaction he will get for a certain behavior. As with children, consistency is essential.

Training (see chapter 6) will provide an intellectual challenge for your new companion. It will give your adopted dog something to think about, and something to do with you, his pack leader. Successes in training will help your dog gain confidence in himself and, in turn, confidence in you and his new home.

Tips for bonding with your dog

- Spend time together - play together.
- Let your dog sleep in your bedroom.
- Tie the dog to you for a couple of hours a day as you go about your business so he knows that you are the leader.
- Feed your dog by hand the first few bites of his dinner or a special treat.
- Smile at your dog and talk in a kind voice.

ADVANTAGES OF ADOPTING A SECOND-HAND DOG

House training is something every dog has to learn. Households whose members are busy with work and school sometimes have a hard time being around for this important task. The second-hand dog will usually be housebroken. It will also not be crying at night or generally needing as much attention as a puppy. As well, it will be past the early inoculations and deworming and its shots will be up-to-date when you get it from the shelter or rescue group. It will not be mouthing with sharp puppy teeth. In other words, you get to skip some of the trying parts of puppyhood and get on with the companionship of an adult dog.

A further advantage of adopting a dog past the puppy stage is that you can see what the pup has become. You can evaluate size, personality, activity level and grooming requirements. You can choose a dog that will fit into the kind of life you lead.

Second-hand dogs are often much less expensive than dogs bought from breeders and pet stores. Shelters usually charge a moderate fee that covers the spaying or neutering or includes a coupon for having it done. Private individuals looking for a new home for a dog often charge something to make sure the adopting person is serious enough about the dog to be willing to pay for it.

PROBLEMS WITH SECOND-HAND DOGS

Some dogs that come into shelters have gone through some unpleasant experiences. Some have been shuffled from place to place or been on their own as strays. These dogs might suffer, on average, from more behavioral problems than dogs that have been raised in a stable environment. They might also have health problems that have gone untreated. You might have to work harder to gain the trust of one of these dogs and give it extra patience. However, some people report wonderful stories of the blossoming of a dog who has never had a good home, but is taken in by a person with a lot of love to give. Some people even adopt dogs with disabilities and find them to be wonderful and rewarding companions.

CHAPTER FOUR

Picking a new puppy

PUPPY PERSONALITIES

In a litter of pups, there will be some that have more dominant personalities, while others are more submissive. Dogs evolved as pack animals and these patterns of dominance and submission serve to maintain pack order. In general, the more dominant puppy will be more aggressive. It will be involved in wrestling with littermates, actively playing with toys and behaving in a manner that might seem hyperactive. It might be the first one to come over when you are introduced to the litter. This pup will be the one chewing another's ear or leg, bumping against other pups or holding them down.

There might be two dominant puppies, though one will probably show more pronounced traits. These dominant puppies will need an owner with a strong personality, able to give decisive direction and take charge. The most dominant pup will attempt to take over the job of family leader and, without proper training, can make life miserable. This dog will often have trouble yielding authority to the younger human members of the family. The second in line in the litter also needs firm training, but is somewhat more accepting of direction. Dogs with these dominance traits can be wonderful animals with someone who knows how to handle them, but are not suitable for an inexperienced or easygoing dog-owner.

There will be puppies in the litter that are moderate in several ways. These middle-of-the-road pups will be more moderately active. They will defend themselves if attacked, but will not initiate the wrestling sessions. These well-balanced, easygoing dogs will be the easiest to train. They will not usually have the problems associated with the highly dominant or highly submissive dogs. This category of puppy personality fits most easily into the average home, especially families with younger children. This is the kind of pup to choose if you are just starting out as a dog-owner.

Some pups are more timid, less active and more watchful. They do not join in wrestling matches and don't even defend themselves all that well when the more dominant pups come after them. The most submissive pups are withdrawn, fearful of encounters with littermates and fearful when meeting new people. The very sensitive puppy will not do well with strict or harsh discipline, but will need extra doses of patience. Puppies that have suffered from unkind treatment, as is often the case with abandoned litters and with some shelter puppies, will need very gentle handling. They are not well suited to homes with small children. If you take a very submissive puppy, you must be willing to give extra time and attention to building up the pup's confidence.

PUPPY TESTS

There are certain quick tests you can perform to indicate the level of dominance of puppies. One test involves picking the pup just off the ground (gently, hands under ribcage) to see how it handles being put in a helpless position. The dominant pup will struggle a lot, the medium pup will relax after a brief struggle and the submissive pup will assume the tail-tucked, ears-back position and perhaps even tremble. A similar range of reactions will be seen if the pup is cradled in the arms like a baby or held down gently when it is lying on its back. The best puppy reaction to sustained petting is relaxation and enjoyment.

A good response to some action or movement on your part, such as clapping your hands, is attention and interest. Lack of interest might indicate a dog that has its own agenda and doesn't care about yours. Some dogs seem to be more interested in dog affairs than in people. The interested dog will pay attention during training and care about pleasing its owner, which is the basis of training. Cowering or running away is the behavior of a fearful, submissive dog that would have a hard time concentrating on training.

These personality tests are best done a little before eight weeks of age because pups seem to go through a skittish time around that age. If you are close enough to the breeder for it to be practical, visit a week or more before you will be picking your pup. The breeder will decide when the pups are old enough to meet strangers. She will also be able to tell you how the personalities are developing and which puppies are fitting into which categories. Breeders usually mark the pups with different colors to help tell them apart and learn their personalities.

THE BEST AGE TO GET A PUP

The best time to get a puppy is between eight and 12 weeks. Before eight weeks, the pup has not had time enough with its mother and littermates to learn proper doggie interaction. The period in the puppy's life from five to 12 weeks is a crucial one for socialization. Contact with other dogs and people will set the puppy up for a life of learning and relationships with both. Puppies who have contact only with their littermates for too long, without good human socialization, will tend to orient to the dog pack, lessening their ability to bond with people. The period from seven to 10 weeks of age is important for environmental enrichment. Be wary of a pup that has been in a kennel very much during this crucial time. Its sense of exploration and learning could be badly stunted.

OFF TO A HEALTHY START

If you have picked your breeder carefully, you will be able to trust that person to have healthy pups. If there are pups whose health is not reliable enough, the breeder will not make them available to you. Wherever you get your pup, you should know the signs of good health. The skin should be clear, with no rashes or scabs. In a healthy pup, the coat will be fluffy, not glossy or greasy, the eyes bright and free of discharge and the ears clean and odor-free. You will hear puppy barks and yips from the healthy pup, but prolonged whining is not a good sign. Be careful of a pup that is much smaller than its littermates.

A very important person in the life of the dog owner is the veterinarian. You should make an appointment for your pup to see the vet as soon as possible after you pick it up. That way, any health problems can be detected quickly. If there is a very serious condition, you might want to return the pup to the breeder before you get attached to it. A pup from a shelter will have been checked by a vet and given its shots before it is allowed out of the shelter. Nevertheless, a visit to *your* vet - the one you will be using regularly - will set your new pup up for a healthier life and add to your peace of mind. If you are in the position of possibly adopting a stray off the street, you should not be surprised to find all sorts of problems. The best advice is for you and your stray to see the vet as soon as possible.

CHAPTER FIVE

Starting out with your new dog

BRINGING YOUR NEW DOG HOME

The first order of business when you get your new dog, from whatever source, is a trip to the vet. The breeder or shelter will have told you what inoculations the puppy has had. The vet will assess your pup's health and tell you when to come back for the additional shots in the series that all puppies need to have (see chapter 10).

What about the trip home from the breeder or shelter? You want it to be as relaxed as possible for everyone, so you should know what to expect. Carsickness and soiling on the part of a puppy or new dog are common, so be prepared. Cover the back seat of the car with a sheet or spread and take along absorbent towels to mop up. There should be someone besides the driver to tend to the puppy. Speaking softly to the pup or singing to it while travelling can be soothing. A box lined with soft towels will be a secure nest for the pup. Avoid any unnecessary lurches with the car and remain as calm and encouraging as possible.

At home, you should have prepared one room for receiving the new dog. There should be a bed, food and water dishes, and a welcoming toy or two. Remove anything the pup could break or he might hurt himself with. Try not to overwhelm the newcomer with attention all at once. The whole experience of going to a new home can be quite unsettling. Children should be warned not to rush over or grab, but to wait patiently for the puppy to come to them. This same advice applies equally to an older dog brought into the home.

Everything that happens with your puppy is part of his training. The puppy is learning from what he sees, hears, tastes and experiences. The relationship you will have with your dog starts the minute you pick him up. If there is any chance for you to have some time off work to spend with your new dog, take it. You will be repaid many times over in the pleasure you can take in a well-adjusted dog that has bonded with you. At the very least, try to get the puppy at the beginning of the weekend so you will have a couple of full days. (For one thing, you might not be getting a full night's sleep for the first little while.)

For the first day, expect your dog to be disoriented. Everything is new and confusing and besides, for a pup, she is missing her mother and littermates. The new arrival might not eat the first day. Don't worry. Just offer the food and stand back. If the food is refused, offer it again after a while. Remember to take the puppy outside for her bathroom break or to the newspapers you have put down for that purpose. It's best to do this after feeding or after a long session of play. Then praise your dog for proper elimination.

Where should your dog sleep? For the very young puppy, a towel-lined box by your bed might be the best solution. If the puppy cries, and it surely will, you can hang a hand down into the box to comfort her. Be prepared to get up and take your dog to her bathroom spot, then put her back to bed more than once during the night. Be gentle and patient and you will be rewarded for your kindness. After a couple of nights, your new dog can be moved to her crate or corral.

HOUSE TRAINING

If your new dog is an older dog, he will probably be house trained already. There is little chance, however, that the eight-week-old pup you have just brought home will head for the back door when he is ready to do his business. House training your dog is a matter of working with the dog's natural inclination not to mess its own sleeping area. If you confine the dog to his own area, such as a crate, or playpen (rigid wire sections that sit directly on the floor and form a corral), during those iffy times when he might sneak off and wet on the living room carpet, you are on your way. Dogs will normally be stimulated to eliminate after eating, so you will want to take the pup outside for his bathroom break right after each meal and at other regular intervals, too. Choose a command to give your dog as you wait for him to choose the right spot. "Hurry up," is sometimes used, though you might find yourself using the phrase in other contexts with unwanted results. "Parktime" is the phrase used by some blind people with their guide dogs. Just keep the word consistent and praise your dog when he performs. (And never scold your dog for messes - this will just confuse him.)

One schedule for this training is:

- First thing in the morning, encourage the pup to follow you to the designated potty place, give the command and praise for performance if it occurs.
- Feed the pup breakfast, then go back to potty place for a second round.
- Leave the pup unconfined to play where you can see him, since this is a relatively safe time, accident-wise. If you must be gone, put the pup in the crate.
- Repeat the process for lunch and dinner: potty, feed, potty, play, nap in crate.
- Bedtime - repeat the routine and put the pup to bed in his crate, but be prepared to get up at night if the pup wakes you up. The pup is telling you he needs to go out. This is what you want. Sooner or later, your pup will sleep through the night.

If you are gone from home for more than three or four hours and cannot get someone to come in for the pup's toileting, expect some messes. You must, in these circumstances, give your pup a bigger area than just his crate, and access to food and water.

If you choose not to use a crate or corral, you still need to keep a close eye on your pup and have a small area you can line with newspapers for when you are gone. You will sometimes be able to anticipate the pup's actions enough to get him outside in time, but accidents will happen. You should just tell the pup "no," take him to the chosen potty place and not scold. Use newspapers only when necessary. If outside is to be your dog's potty place, use it from the beginning as much as possible.

Here are six keys to good house training for a pup or an older dog coming into your home:

- Establish a routine. Dogs thrive on routine.
- Feed on a schedule as much as possible.
- Praise your dog when he does the right thing.
- Keep an eye on your dog. Correct at the time of the mistake.
- Get rid of the odor of past mistakes.
- Be patient.

Since there will probably be a few accidents no matter how careful you are with house training, it is good to be able to clean up efficiently. Don't use any cleaner containing ammonia since its smell is similar to urine - it will reinforce the smell and mark the spot as one that should be used again. An acid such as household white vinegar, in a weak warm water solution with a little dishwashing detergent, makes a good cleanup liquid. There are also commercial products specifically for the purpose that contain neutralizing enzymes.

START GOOD HABITS EARLY

There are a number of routines you will want to start when your dog is young. Getting your dog accustomed to being handled is very important. You will need to make regular examinations yourself and tend to grooming needs. You don't want a dog that resents or is nervous of handling.

Social skills also need development. Make sure that your young dog is exposed to people of all ages, sizes and descriptions (with the warning that public places can have dangerous germs for the pup that has not had the full series of inoculations and you should try to socialize in safer places with vaccinated dogs). Try to arrange for pleasant encounters with people, other dogs and family pets. In the case of some breeds, such as herding types, you will be attempting to overcome the natural suspiciousness that has been bred into the dog for centuries. Act as if it is natural for your dog to be confident and friendly. Don't encourage shyness by cuddling or soothing the dog if it shows shyness. Take your dog for car rides regularly. Early carsickness is usually outgrown as confidence increases.

Don't let the cuteness of a young dog cause you to tolerate behavior that you will not find cute later. Destruction of property and chewing people's hands should never be allowed. Stern reprimands and distraction with alternative items are both proper responses. You will need the co-operation of every member of the household and even visiting friends in order to maintain the ground rules that you establish. Otherwise, the dog will be confused. Don't let children tease the dog or roughhouse as if they were all pups. Humans must be above the dog in social standing, regardless of age. Any signs of guarding food or toys must be dealt with early. The dog must submit to its food or toys being taken away without signs of aggression. Some trainers recommend a stern verbal correction and *banishment to the crate* or playpen as an effective response. Continued infractions call for a gentle scruff shake (see chapter 6 on training).

Introduce your young dog to the leash by 10 weeks or so. Keep the exercise casual and fun, praising the pup when she follows you, but not forcing the issue right away. Use a lightweight leash for the young dog even if you need to buy a stronger one for later.

Talk to your dog. Dogs are capable of understanding human words and will find it intellectually stimulating to learn some. You can build your dog's vocabulary the way you would teach a child, with clear and simple speech. Most dogs develop their own collection of known words, often relating to food and recreation.

EQUIPMENT

A very useful piece of equipment for the dog owner is the crate. Though the crate was originally designed for animal transport, it has earned a place in many homes because of its practical uses. Some crates are all metal and quite open, while others are solid metal or plastic. Dogs who are accustomed to them from an early age find them safe and comforting, like a cozy den. The crate is good for keeping your dog confined in an airplane or automobile (see chapter 11 on travel), but also keeps your pooch out from under foot at home when necessary and is a useful tool for housebreaking.

Before you buy a crate, you need to realize that there are several grades and some are not strong enough for air shipping. The proper crate size for your dog is one that will allow it to stand up, lie down and turn around comfortably when it has attained its adult size. Unfortunately, such a roomy crate might tempt a puppy to soil it, so a divider should be used while the dog is small.

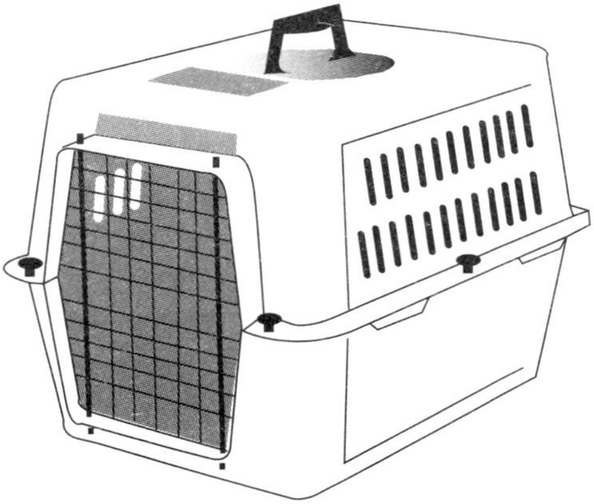

Another useful piece of equipment for the puppy owner is the **baby gate**. It allows you to confine the pup to the area that is safer, or more easily cleaned. If the pup cannot be right with you, it can at least see you and can enjoy your company without getting underfoot. The gates with two moving screened sections are much safer than the old expandable accordion type.

Food and water bowls are essential equipment for your dog. They are available in various materials including ceramic, plastic and stainless steel. Rubber rims at the bottom are useful to prevent sliding and dishes that are wider at the bottom are harder to upset. The stainless-steel bowl is a good choice because it is very durable, puts nothing into the food or water and is easy to keep clean. Specially designed dishes with narrow tops keep the ears of long-eared dogs out of their food and water. (You appreciate the significance of this idea best after you have had a long-eared dog.)

Collars and leashes are must-have items. They are an essential part of the training process and will be discussed again in the chapter on training. There are several designs of each. The buckle or snap collar, with identification tags attached (and taped if they jingle) is what your dog will wear every day. Each collar is adjustable to some extent. The properly adjusted collar will allow you to slide two fingers between the collar and your dog's neck. For the short-haired dog, the collar can be either rolled or flat. Long-haired dogs fare better with the rolled collar as it disrupts the direction of the long neck ruff hair less than a flat collar.

Strong, serviceable collars are available in leather and nylon webbing. The nylon takes washing better than leather, which can absorb doggy odor permanently, but loses its suppleness with washing. A newer innovation - the snap fastener - replaces the buckle on some collars, and works very well. It releases easily with a firm squeeze even when the collar is under tension. This is a convenience at bathtime and a life-saver in emergencies. A buckle can be hard to undo on a panicky, struggling dog whose collar has become caught on something. For the very small dog, a harness might be the better choice, since some of the tiny breeds have delicate windpipes. Chain-slip collars will be discussed in the section on training because they should be used only under strict supervision. They are a serious hazard for the unattended dog.

Leashes come in various materials: leather, nylon or cotton webbing and chain. The advantage of the chain leash is that it is not nice to chew. Dogs should never be allowed to chew their leashes. The chain can, however, be annoyingly noisy and uncomfortable in the hand if you should want to take up some of the slack. A 2 m (6 ft.) leash is a good all-purpose length and is the one specified in some city by-laws.

Your dog will appreciate a **bed** of its own. There are plastic beds, wicker beds with pads and floppy beanbag beds. A washable cover is a good idea. Some beanbags have cedar filling to help deodorize.

Grooming tools vary with the coat of the dog (see chapter 7 on grooming). The basic grooming kit will include a bristle brush for the fine coat, and a comb with widely spaced teeth to help remove tangles in longer hair, as well as burrs and other debris. Nail clippers are also a necessity. You don't want to be having the vet trim your dog's nails every time you visit.

Dogs enjoy chewing and some **toys** are designed to put this trait to good use. Nylon bones (in a size too big to swallow) exercise the jaws and help clean your dog's teeth. Squeaky toys are sometimes appealing since they mimic the noises dogs associate with prey. Amazingly, many dogs do not seem to tear up the very delicate rubber squeaky toys. However, if your dog should, take the pieces away before the pieces or the squeakers get swallowed.

Some dogs chew up and swallow pieces of knotted string toys and large chunks of rawhide bones. Neither of these is good to have passing through the digestive tract. Some balls are small enough to get stuck in the throat with fatal results. The dyes in fluorescent colored tennis balls might not be safe for dogs to chew. You would be well advised to give your dog only balls (again, large enough not to be choking hazards) designed for dogs since they should be safe to chew. Hollow hard-rubber toys that can be stuffed with something like peanut butter can be a wonderful distraction. Stuffed animals are favorites because dogs like to shake them like prey. You will be picking up the stuffing from the carpet, but the dog will be having fun.

CHAPTER SIX

Training your dog

A well-trained dog is a good citizen, well behaved and reliable. She does not bark all night, pull you down the street by the leash or jump up on your friends. An untrained dog, on the other hand, can be a real nuisance. An untrained dog lacks a good working relationship with his owner, a relationship that should give the dog much security. An untrained (or incorrectly trained) dog can be destructive and even dangerous. Think of training as a gift you give your dog. You care enough to spend the time and effort so your dog can become a good citizen.

When it comes to training your dog, the best approaches are:

- Attend group classes.
- Have individual instruction for you and your dog.
- Hire a trainer to work with your dog and then include some instruction for you.

If you have a dog that you are afraid of, you need to find a good professional trainer. Aggression in dogs, especially large dogs, is a serious matter. The number of injuries and even deaths from dog attacks is alarmingly high. If you are not sure how aggressive your dog might be, a trainer can help you assess the situation and decide what course to take.

You might be interested in more formal obedience activities. There are many opportunities to participate in activities with your dog, many sponsored by kennel clubs and local dog groups. Some of these are described in chapter 13 on having fun with your dog.

TRAINING BASICS

Dogs in the wild live in packs in which a strong leader, known as the alpha, is responsible for pack order. Dogs have evolved to live with such a system. A dog that lives with humans can accept its human companion as pack leader if the human takes the lead. Without a strong human leader, the dog steps in and takes the position itself. You need not be harsh with your dog, in most cases, to be the leader of the family pack. You must, however, never waiver in your conviction that you are the boss.

Challenges from your dog must be met firmly and consistently. The other members of the family must also be above the dog in status, or the dog will not respect them properly. Think of your dog as a well-loved low man on the totem pole. If you approach the subject of training with enthusiasm and the desire to better the human-dog relationship, you will have the best chance for success. You must also remember that training is an ongoing process that will flavor all activities you have with your dog, since learning goes on whether a formal lesson is in progress or not.

If your dog is having a hard time accepting you as pack leader, you might try an exercise that imitates the behavior of wild dogs, called the shake-down. Use it *only* after the dog has committed a serious offense that seems clearly an attempt to usurp power. To do the shake-down, you take hold of the skin on either side of the neck (or the scruff of the neck in a small dog) and give the dog a good shake, back and forth while maintaining eye contact and saying the word "no" in a low growly voice. With many dogs, this approach will never be needed, but with some it will be essential to maintain your status as pack leader. Do not try the shake-down with a dog you are afraid of. In such a case, consult a professional trainer.

Basic approaches to training

There are two basic approaches to dog training. You do not have to choose one exclusively over the other, but rather, can incorporate certain elements of each as needed. The first method of training involves punishment, or correction, ranges from a mild swat on the muzzle or rump to some pretty aggressive tactics that are used by professional trainers in extreme cases. (Understand that some other trainers do not approve of such harsh techniques.) The standard, widely accepted correction is administered by way of a quick jerk and release on a tightening or training collar. Some trainers feel that the same leash jerk is just as effective on a standard leather buckle or nylon collar. Remember that these aggressive techniques must be timed properly and administered consistently. They're not for beginners.

The second training approach uses positive methods such as rewards to reinforce desired behavior. The rewards can be verbal (praise), physical (petting) or some sort of food treat.

Both of these methods depend on association. Your dog associates discomfort with doing the wrong thing, or reward with doing the right thing. Corrections have the desired effect, however, only if administered when the dog is doing the behavior. A dog does not have the ability to associate the correction with an action in the past.

Discomfort avoidance or punishment can work quickly, but can cause anxiety in some dogs. Submissive or soft dogs can be broken completely with harsh treatment, and aggressive dogs can become more aggressive. The more positive approach of the reward system tends to build confidence in a dog and enhance its relationship with the owner. Some trainers like to give the dog the chance to respond to a gentler approach and then progress to some stronger form of correction if they feel the dog has understood a concept, but is stubbornly refusing to comply with a command.

TIPS BEFORE YOU START

Try to have a good attitude about the training. Think of yourself and your dog as a team working together, with you as the captain. Be generous with praise when your dog does something right. Let your affection for your dog show with your voice, body language and smile. Your dog can find pleasure in pleasing you. Even if corrections are necessary, they can be done in the spirit of building a good working relationship. Quiet dogs respond well to more lavish praise, while excitable dogs might do better with milder expressions of approval.

Be clear and be consistent. Speak the command word clearly

(avoid any whiny or questioning tone of voice) and use the same word for the command every time. Remember to say "sit" and not "sit down," since "down" is another command altogether. If you want your dog to get off the sofa, say "off," not "get down," or the dog might hear and obey "down."

Say the command one time and have it obeyed. Once you give the command, make sure your dog obeys, even if you have to guide your dog into position. Then praise your dog. Allowing a dog *not* to obey a command is a very strong lesson that you don't really want your dog to learn.

Since dogs think of looking as an aggressive act (in the wild, they do not stare at the alpha), you need to get your dog used to looking at you. When you say your dog's name, the dog should look at you for instructions. Praise such "looking" behavior. You might have to seat your dog in front of you and draw attention to your eyes, saying "look" or "watch me" and give praise for compliance.

You should also choose a word to use when you are finished with a certain command and the dog is released from obeying it. It is the equivalent of the "at ease" command. The command should be something you do not say frequently in conversation, and should be used consistently.

At some point, you will want to work without a leash. You should have a fenced-in area if possible. You should be aware that even very obedient and well-trained dogs have been known to take off on their trainers or owners, sometimes with serious or tragic results.

MINIMAL TRAINING

While dog trainers can train animals to do everything we see in movies and on TV, real families often opt for minimal training. Here's a bare-bones minimum that should begin at the puppy stage:

- **House training** You don't want your dog doing his business in the house.
- **Name** Your dog should look at you when his name is called.

- **Sit** To gain control.
- **Stay** So your dog doesn't run out into traffic.
- **No** To stop whatever your dog is doing now.
- **Come** To call your dog back to you.

A little firm training, rewards for good behavior and a stern "no" when your dog gets it wrong should make this easy. For more sophisticated training, you and your dog really should take a class.

Training collars

There are many kinds of collars for dogs. Your dog's everyday collar will be one of those described in the chapter on starting out with your dog. It should not ever be a collar that tightens on the dog's neck. Such collars are reserved for training sessions and are removed afterwards, as they are a strangulation hazard. The purpose of the training collar - sometimes called the slip collar, check chain or choke collar - is to administer an unpleasant physical sensation to the dog as a correction for an inappropriate action. The slip collar is designed to deliver pressure on the dog's neck for a very short length of time and then release. To do this, the collar must be put on in the right way. Improper use can hurt the dog. The correct way to put it on is to have the chain in the shape

of the letter P with the back of the P on top and the stem facing you. The tightening action of the chain will be on back of the neck and not on the throat and delicate windpipe.

The P shape is formed by holding one of the large circles at each end and dropping the length of the chain through the circle you are holding to form a loop. Slip collars are also available in nylon cord and in metal with prongs that press into the dog's neck when the leash is jerked. These "prong" collars are usually used only with large powerful strong-necked dogs that need extra control and should not be necessary with proper training.

Teaching the sit

Have the dog stand in front of you, facing sideways, and hold the leash near the collar. Kneel and press on your dog's back in front of the hip bone, and give the command with your dog's name first, then "sit." Your dog should respond to the pressure by sitting. Hold your dog in position for a few seconds, telling him how wonderful he is, then use the release word and let him get up. Praise your dog and repeat the procedure as he comes to associate the word "sit" with the action. Another training approach is to "tuck" the dog into position by pushing on the back of its knees and folding the legs forward. A third method is to have your dog standing with his side to you and move a treat or toy over his head so that he sits automatically as he lifts his head to keep an eye on the item.

Teaching the sit-stay

With your dog in the sit position at your left, bring your hand in front of her face, palm towards the dog, and say, simply, "stay." Then step directly in front of your dog, holding the leash taut above her head to prevent forward motion, and repeat the command word, "stay." Keep eye contact with your dog while blocking her path for a few seconds. Then return to the side position, release and praise. Increase the time that your dog is required to hold the stay position. When a half a minute of attentive staying is accomplished, with the taut leash, let the leash go slack for a bit of the stay, then resume the taut leash for the finish up. Increase the loose leash time, reinforcing your dog's attention with the command word stay, if the dog seems about to move. You are working up to being able to back off further and further from the dog, eventually laying the leash down on the ground with your foot on it. Any failure should put you back to up-close or taut leash exercises. Verbal corrections can be used for a while, after which more physical corrections, such as leading the dog back to the spot where it is supposed to be, might be necessary. Tough, dominant dogs require harsher means, while milder dogs will usually respond to mild reprimands.

Teaching the recall "come"

The recall command (come when called) is a vital one for your dog to learn. It is good idea to teach it and practice it often. It's a good idea not to let this command become associated with unpleasant events. If you use the command to get your dog to come for his bath, and your dog doesn't relish baths, the association is not going to be a good one. Use the recall command to call him for dinner, or playtime. Welcome your dog with joy and open arms when he comes to you when called. Even if you have had a hard time getting your dog to come to you, never scold him when he comes.

One of the techniques for teaching the recall is to have your dog walking casually ahead of you and then give the leash a very quick jerk and call to him, with his name first, and then the command "come!" Then you proceed to take a few quick steps backward and squat. This action is an invitation to your dog to chase you. Reward your dog with praise, a toy or a treat. Repeat. As the training continues, you will stop squatting, and then reduce the number of backward steps until there are none. You will also begin to guide your dog, by way of the leash, into a sitting position in front of you.

For the next step in recall, have your dog stay in the sitting position and back off to the end of the leash. Then call excitedly, giving the leash a quick jerk the first few times you try the exercise. You might have the best success if you use a treat to reward every time at first, then reduce the frequency of treats, while keeping it up just now and then.

Remember - never scold a dog that has just come to you.

Teaching the down-stay

This command might cause some problems with you and your dog if there is any doubt who is the boss. A dog feels vulnerable in the down position and you are taking the dominant role when you demand that your dog lie down. You will be laying your dog down gently but firmly while saying the dog's name and the command word "down." With the dog sitting on your left, relax it by stroking it on the back a few times. Then lift each front leg in turn to let the dog get used to the feel. Next take hold of each of the dog's front paws and slide them forward. Talk soothingly, since this might be disturbing to your dog. You must not allow your dog to put its mouth on you or growl. Mouthing gets the dog a loud verbal reprimand and growling or snapping calls for a scruff shake, as described earlier in this chapter. (Remember - don't try the scruff shake with a large dog you are afraid of. It is just too dangerous.) When the dog can hold the down position for 15 seconds without being touched, use the stay command to keep the dog in that position until released. Larger dogs have to be eased into the down position from the front, drawing both front legs forward until the elbows are on the ground.

There are other methods of teaching the down position. A mild reward method is to hold a treat in front of your dog and then draw her forward and down while pressing on her back and giving the "down" command. Some very co-operative dogs will even learn the "down" command with verbal encouragement and the patting of the floor. A more physical, but much harsher, method has you put the dog's leash under your foot and pull up on the handle of the leash. This pulls the dog downward by the collar. A very stubborn dog might keep its back end in the air though its neck is down, but it will give in eventually if you persist. As mentioned, the down and stay is a test of dominance and, as such, is a useful training tool to reinforce your role as leader.

Teaching the stand

This useful position is taught from the sit. With your dog on your left, take hold of his collar, with the back of your right hand facing his throat. Pull forward while giving the command, name first, then "stand." With your left hand, pull up under his tummy. As your dog rises, repeat the command, praise and pet your dog's back and legs. This command is very useful for vet exams and grooming.

LEASH WALKING

There are times when a nice leisurely walk with your dog does not require the more rigid control involved in walking to heel. It is enough for the dog to walk ahead with the leash slack between you. The way to train your dog not to pull is to let it walk ahead, then pop the leash quickly when the dog begins to pull and give the command "don't pull," "walk nicely" or whatever you choose, as long as it is always the same words. Praise your dog for keeping some slack in the leash and pop the leash when it gets tight, issuing the chosen command. You will want your dog to stop at the curb every time you get to a street. Choose a command - probably "stop" and your dog's name - and give it as the dog gets to the curb. When you decide to continue, give the walk command and go on. Before long the dog will stop automatically.

WALKING AT HEEL

There are circumstances in which only walking at heel is appropriate - a busy city sidewalk is one example. You teach the heel position beginning with the dog sitting on your left. Take up the slack in the leash, holding the excess in your left hand. Give the command "heel" after your dog's name and step off briskly. The dog should be trotting at your side, close to your leg, and keeping his eye on you. The taut leash prevents the dog from straying from your side. With your right hand, you can give occasional treats. After a while, the taut leash can be loosened some. Praise your dog for correct behavior and reduce the frequency of treats. After a while, mild leash corrections can be given if your dog pulls away from the heel position. If you want your dog to sit each time you stop walking, as is traditional in dog training, you can anticipate your stop by a few steps and issue the "sit" command, reaching down to tuck the dog under for the sit. If your dog already knows the "sit" command, the word alone might be enough.

An alternate method for teaching the heel command is to walk with your dog on your left, with the leash somewhat slack, and administer leash corrections (quick jerks on the leash) when the dog strays from the correct position. Corrections should not be too hard or the neck can be injured.

CHAPTER SEVEN

Grooming your dog

Regular tending to the grooming needs of your dog has several advantages. Your dog will be more pleasant to be around, since he'll be clean and relatively free of doggie odor. Your dog will be more comfortable, since he'll be free of skin conditions, mats and burrs. Less dog hair will find its way into your home if it is removed regularly with brushing. You will have the chance to check your dog for abnormalities and deal with them, thus heading off some health problems. Also, you will find that grooming time helps reaffirm your relationship with your dog while giving you some enjoyable time together.

One mark of a healthy, well-cared for dog is a fine coat. The first step in maintaining a fine coat on your dog is to feed him a high-quality diet. Some people use dietary supplements that are high in fat-soluble vitamins. Coat care will include bathing, combing and brushing, and trimming, clipping or stripping.

BATHING

Your dog's coat should be kept clean by bathing, but dogs differ greatly in how often they need a bath. Some dogs seem to get smelly quickly, while some go months on end with no odor. Bathing can help eliminate skin parasites and can also provide treatment for skin conditions if medicated shampoos are used. However, bathing also removes a coat of oil that protects your dog from the cold, so bathe only when necessary and keep your pooch warm.

Bathing should be done with lukewarm water (35°C or 95°F), never with cold water from the hose outside. You should first brush your dog and remove any mats before bathing. In the tub or a plastic bath basin, use a rubber mat to prevent slipping. Wet your dog and apply shampoo (canine, preferably, or tearless or what your vet prescribes), following the instructions on the container. Lather and rinse well. Do the body first, then the head; avoid getting the shampoo in the eyes. (The only exception to this rule is if your dog has fleas, in which case you start with the head.) Rinse and dry the head first, then rinse the body. Do yourself and the dog a favor and get a spray nozzle. It is so much faster and easier than any other way.

Grooming Tools

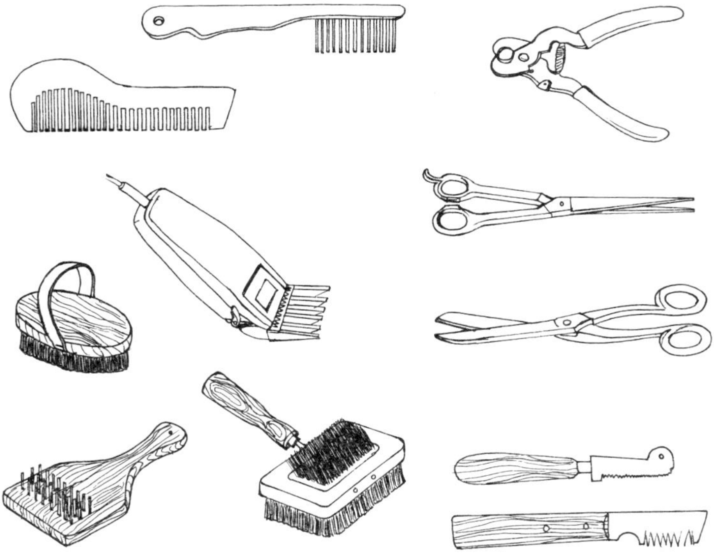

You might find that a conditioner helps your dog's coat. Apply it now and rinse thoroughly. Squeeze out excess moisture from your dog's coat. Dry your dog with a towel, especially inside the ears. Unless the weather is very warm, dry your dog with a hair-dryer set on low. A stand that holds the dryer allows you to use both hands on the coat during drying. This is essential for curly dogs such as Poodles and Bichon Frises that have their coats straightened while drying. Keep an eye on your dog after a bath because this is precisely the time he will go looking for something to roll in to smell like a real dog again. Be careful not to let your dog get chilled, even after he has been dry for a while.

BRUSHING

Brushing removes dirt and dead hair from your dog's coat. For dogs with long coats, use a slicker brush first to untangle the hair, followed by the bristle brush for silky coats such as the Yorkshire Terrier's or a pin brush for rougher fluffier coats such as the Collie's. Metal-tooth curry combs are good for removing the undercoat, which is shed (called blowing coat) each spring or summer. Brush in the direction of the growth of the hair. Be careful that the wire teeth of the slicker do not dig into the dog's skin. Start at the head and work to the tail, followed by the sides of the dog. Tangles are often found behind the ears and under the arms.

If there is matting (tangled masses of hair), it will need to be removed carefully with the brush or cut away with scissors. Try to work the tangles out with your fingers before cutting. Conditioner applied to the mats will make them easier to untangle. Mats really must be dealt with because they are uncomfortable for your dog, hold in heat and moisture and encourage infections known as hot spots. There are special tools for removing stubborn mats. These tools, called mat-splitters, are claw-like combs with blades on one side which actually shred the mats for easier removal. In cases of extensive matting, the dog's coat should be clipped off by a professional groomer.

Short-haired dogs benefit from regular brushing, but do not need daily care. Various pieces of equipment, such as the rubber brush or the hound glove, help loosen hairs and dead skin before the brush removes them. A coat dressing may be used once a week to add sheen and a pleasant smell. Rubbing the dog's coat with a chamois also increases shine.

CLIPPING AND STRIPPING

Dogs with curly and wiry coats require more than brushing to look decent. Curly coats, such as the poodle's, keep growing and need to be clipped every six weeks. Curly breeds have some formal styles of cut for dogs being shown and more casual ones for household pets. The poodle puppy cut, for example, is short and curly all over. Spaniels and Terriers with wiry coats can be clipped, but the show-dog coat is hand stripped with special tools that remove the old hair. It takes several hours to do and requires some practice. Professional grooming is expensive. If you are interested in trying your hand at grooming at home, get some books with detailed instructions, but also think about having a professional give you a demonstration. There are even some dog grooming salons operating now that have all the equipment, grooming stands, bathtubs and dryers for you to groom your dog there.

FOOT CARE

Dogs grow long hair between the pads of their feet and this hair should be kept trimmed. If left long, the hair collects dirt and stones, and ice balls in snowy weather. Trim carefully with scissors to give the foot a clean, rounded appearance. Check between the toes for grass seeds that can cause much discomfort, especially if they sprout. Also check for ice and now in the winter.

Toenails grow continuously and need to be trimmed. For very small dogs, toenail clippers are adequate, but larger dogs' nails require the heavy-duty guillotine-type cutters. The toenail is inserted into the hole and the handle squeezed to move the blade against the toenail. You want to avoid cutting the nail so close as to affect the quick. In white toenails, the quick shows as pink flesh inside the nail. With dark nails, you have to guess how close to cut, and it is best to take off just a little at a time until the nails are short enough. It is a good idea to have blood-clotting powder on hand before you start. Rough edges can be smoothed with a nail file. Dew claws, the extra claws that grow higher up on the front legs, in our thumb position, should be kept trimmed, too, since they can grow long and curl into the flesh.

Tips for making nail clipping easier:

- Get your dog accustomed to having its paws handled. Do it casually when you are not going to cut nails.
- Cut just one nail and give a treat. The next day, do another and work up to doing them all at once.
- Make sure your equipment is sharp. Replacement blades can be bought for the clippers. Keep the clippers clean.
- Be calm yourself. Your attitude is contagious.
- Get some Kwik-Stop to stop bleeding if you should cut into the quick.

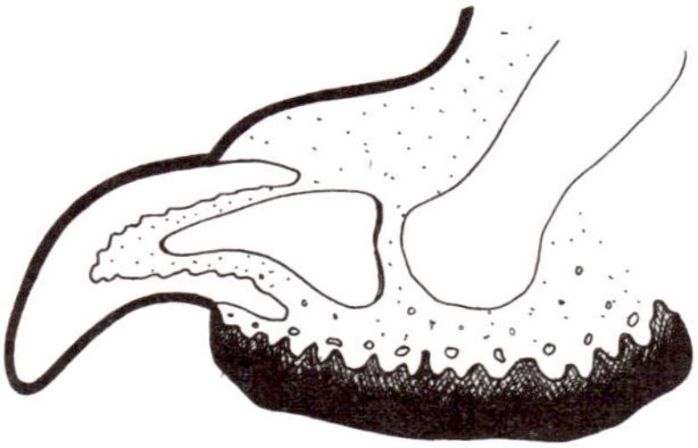

EXPRESSING THE ANAL GLANDS

Dogs have glands on either side of the anus that supply scent for marking territory and other canine communication. Sometimes these glands become impacted and need emptying. Signs of trouble include tail dragging and licking the anal area. The procedure for emptying the glands is to glove your hand, lift the dog's tail, cover the area with a tissue and squeeze firmly but gently on either side of and slightly below the anus. The normal color of what comes out (sometimes with force) is yellowish brown. If you see blood or pus, or need more instruction in the process, ask your vet. Some dogs seem to get along fine without any intervention. Before a bath is a sensible time to check or empty the glands.

TOOTH BRUSHING

Use special canine toothpaste available in pet stores or from your vet. Human toothpaste is not suitable. A soft bristled child's toothbrush works well. If your dog is very unhappy at this approach, start just rubbing your finger over the teeth, then wrap a cloth around your finger and rub. Add toothpaste, baking soda or hydrogen-peroxide mouthwash to the rag. There are also finger covers with little bristles, available at pet stores.

CARING FOR THE FACE

Some breeds, especially those with protruding eyes, have a discharge from the eyes that discolors the fur on the face. The eyes may be bathed with cool water and cotton. Use a different piece of cotton for each eye. Watch for eyelashes or facial hairs curling into the eyes and causing irritation. Any inflammation or pus should be reported to the vet. Ears should be checked for irritation or excess wax and cleaned gently with cotton moistened with mineral oil or alcohol. Heavy hair growth in the ear can cause wax accumulation and should be removed by pulling it out. Check with your vet on this matter. Dogs with deep folds on their faces need these folds cleaned regularly.

CHAPTER EIGHT

Dog nutrition

Just like people, dogs need to eat well and have their nutritional requirements met to grow and thrive. In times past, wild dogs hunted for their food, which mostly consisted of prey consumed whole. The hair, skin and bones, as well as the stomach contents of the prey served up a feast of vitamins, minerals, protein, fat, carbohydrates and fiber. Domesticated dogs in rural areas continue to make use of such foods as they clean mice from barns and crunch the occasional squirrel. Many pets today, however, are completely dependent on their owners for nutrition and it is your job to make sure that your dog's diet has everything necessary for optimum health.

KINDS OF DOG FOOD

Basically, the three kinds of dog food are dry, semi-moist and canned. Each contains much the same main ingredients, but there are some important differences. Semi-moist is the least desirable in that it requires a high level of preservatives to keep it from spoiling. It is often dyed bright red and dressed up to look like hamburger meat. The food coloring, preservatives and the high level of sugar some products contain make them a poor bet.

Dry dog food, sometimes called kibble, comes in several grades or levels of quality. The lowest (generic economy brands) are made with poor ingredients and are not highly digestible. As well, they (and some more expensive brands, too) often contain preservatives such as BHT and BHA or a suspect substance called ethoxyquin. Standard grocery-store brands usually have better ingredients than the economy dog foods, but do not contain the higher-quality food sources found in the premium brands sold at pet stores and veterinary clinics. These premium brands are more expensive, but are more digestible, so serving sizes can be smaller. In some "super premium" brands, often available through mail order, the protein sources are foods considered fit for human consumption. Preservatives in better brands tend to be natural nutrients such as vitamin E or vitamin C.

Dry dog food is made by mixing ingredients into a homogeneous dough that is then extruded into the desired shape and baked. The pieces are then sprayed with fat to enhance their flavor and add this needed nutrient. For better mixing, the ingredients are in powder or meal form, including the meat, if any.

Meat meal is one of the protein sources for dry dog food. The meat meal used in many brands is made by grinding, cooking and drying material from rendered animal parts from various sources and species, almost all of which have been rated as unfit for human consumption. This means that the meat used could be from diseased animals, past the best-before date or otherwise unacceptable. Only the super premium dog foods use meat that is fit for humans.

There has been some concern as to what goes into some pet foods. Meat by-products include feet, beaks and feathers, in the case of chickens, as well as all internal organs. The grains that supply carbohydrates can also be of inferior grades, even spoiled by mold.

Of course, dry dog food has the advantage of convenience. It is light and does not require refrigeration. Disadvantages include spoiling by insects, vermin or water, the high level of processing that can reduce the level of nutrients, the low level of fat and thus calories, and the problem of the fat going rancid. Dry kibble is usually formulated to be a complete diet.

Canned products require no preservatives, since the canning process eliminates spoiling agents. Other advantages include their palatability, digestibility and durability. On the other side, canned dog food is heavy, contains a lot of water and requires refrigeration after opening. Canned meat by itself is not a complete diet. Canned products designed to be complete diets often contain vegetable and grain ingredients along with some protein source, much the same as dry foods, and usually have added vitamins and minerals. Foods which are labeled as complete and balanced must conform to standards set out by the Association of American Feed Control Officers or the Canadian Veterinary Medical Association. Look for the seals of these organizations on the package labels.

READING LABELS

Since there is so much variation in quality, ingredients and price, you must look carefully at labels to know what you're buying. Product labels list ingredients in order of amount, most to least, or with specific percentages. However, sometimes manufacturers split one ingredient into two types in the listing, so that it does not show up as the first ingredient. You must consider the top three ingredients to see what the *main* ingredient really is. Even with such labeling, consumers are not getting the whole story, since some nutrients vary in how much is usable and how much passes through the dog's system unused. High-quality proteins - such as those from muscle and internal organs - are more usable than those from various ingredients listed as animal by-products.

SUPPLEMENTING YOUR DOG'S DIET

Though dog foods labeled as complete are designed to give your dog all the nutrients she needs, you might want to supplement your dog's diet with foods chosen to provide certain nutrients or beneficial effects. Avoid, of course, giving your dog "people foods" that are sweet, salty, greasy or highly processed.

People foods that are not good for your dog include:

- sweet baked goods such as cookies and cake
- salty foods such as potato chips
- greasy foods such as bacon, ham, wieners
- sweets such as candies, especially chocolate, which can be poisonous
- sweet beverages such as pop; any alcoholic beverages

Use fresh foods that provide vitamins and enzymes. Garlic has been cited as having health benefits for people as well as dogs, and dogs seem to really like it. You can chop up a half a clove and add it to your dog's regular dinner. (Don't go overboard

- garlic can cause problems at high levels.) While milk can cause diarrhea, yogurt can be safely added to your dog's diet and cottage cheese is an easily digestible source of protein. Scraps of fresh raw beef and lamb (from a reliable source), with most of the fat trimmed away, can be added in small amounts. Poultry should be cooked, since contamination is not uncommon in uncooked chicken and turkey. Organ meats such as liver, kidney and heart have valuable nutrients, but keep the liver portions small. Egg is the best-quality protein available. Cooked whole eggs and raw yolks are beneficial, but raw whites should be given only now and then. Fresh fruits and vegetables add vitamins and fiber, and dogs are often very fond of them. Avoid cabbage because of its gas-producing qualities and onions because of the anemia associated with them (as described further on). Fresh foods supply your dog with important enzymes and other nutrients that are lost in dog-food processing. The recommended amount of commercial food should be reduced a bit to allow for the added calories from the supplementation.

COOKING FOR YOUR DOG

It is possible to prepare you dog's entire diet yourself, but if you do, it is essential to do it right. Get a book that deals specifically with home-prepared canine diets and study it carefully. A mix of lean meats, organ meats, other protein sources such as cottage cheese or eggs, carbohydrates such as grains, and vegetables will make up a well-balanced diet. Calcium supplementation will be necessary. Raw vegetables are good and should be grated for better use of the nutrients. Some dogs really love fruit, too. Share some of that orange you're eating.

It need not be all that hard to prepare your dog's dinner. If you are cooking meat, you can take a portion out and cook it simply without onions (use garlic) for the dog while cooking your own meal however you like. The rice you are eating and the cooked carrots will be perfect for your canine friend. When you scramble eggs for yourself, they can be the protein part of your dog's breakfast. Oatmeal is nice for pooches, too, with some fruit and yogurt.

Any changes to your dog's diet should be gradual. Mix in the new food in a small proportion for a while, increasing little by little until the change is complete. New puppies should be fed the same food the breeder was using and changed by this method if change is desired.

When choosing foods for your dog, avoid fatty, salty and sweet items. Think simple and fresh - such as grated vegetables and fruit and lean raw meat. Choose the carrot over the doughnut.

SPECIAL FEEDING CIRCUMSTANCES

There are special circumstances in the life of a dog that call for special feeding. Puppies need extra nutrition (except for some large breeds for whom extra nutrition causes them to grow too fast) to form their growing bodies, and nursing mothers need more food to supply milk for their pups. Highly active working and sporting dogs need foods with higher proportions of protein, fat and carbohydrates, but they should not be fed immediately before or after intense activity. There are conflicting opinions as to the protein needs of older dogs. Individual dogs age differently, as do people. Your vet will be able to advise you what your particular dog will likely need.

THE PROBLEM OF TOO MUCH WEIGHT

You will not be surprised to hear that the overweight dog will suffer health problems related to obesity. Excess weight contributes to increased risk of heart and lung problems, high blood pressure, susceptibility to disease, anaesthetic and surgical problems, heatstroke, shortened life span and reproductive problems. Though some breeds of dogs have a genetic predisposition to gaining excessive weight, the problem is usually that the owner is feeding too much. Sometimes the extra calories come from treats that are not good for your dog anyway, such as sugary baked goods. The problem is often aggravated by too little exercise.

But how can you know if your dog is overweight? Your vet is

your best source of advice on this question, but an easy test will give you some indication. When you hold your dog, you should be able to feel his ribs easily, with just a very light layer of fat under the skin.

What is the solution to excess weight? More activity and fewer calories; cut food intake by about a fifth and increase your dog's level of physical activity.

FOODS TO AVOID

Besides the fatty, spicy or salty foods mentioned above, there are other foods that you should absolutely avoid feeding to your dog. Though onions are good for human dining, they have a very bad effect on dogs and some other animals. Cooked and raw onions both contain chemicals that oxidize red blood cells and cause anemia.

Chocolate can cause very serious and immediate problems for your dog. This favorite of humans contains caffeine and theobromine, members of the harmful chemical group called methylxanthines. The darker the chocolate, the more powerful the ill effects on your dog. Even one square of baker's chocolate can kill a small dog.

Very large quantities of liver can overdose a dog on vitamin A, so keep this treat to tidbits.

While large beef knuckle bones are reasonably safe, bones from chicken and pork, as well as the sharp, slender bones of steaks, are not hard enough to withstand the powerful jaws of a dog. Small pieces can splinter off and cause choking or internal damage.

Remember, no chocolate, no onions, no chicken, pork or steak bones and easy on the liver.

OTHER NUTRITIONAL ELEMENTS

A very important element in your dog's nutrition is clean, fresh water. Give your dog water from the same source you drink from yourself and clean the water dish every day. Your dog will require more water when he eats dry food. The food dish should have leftover food removed and be cleaned frequently as well.

Dog owners sometimes wonder about vitamin supplements. Some vitamins can cause serious or fatal results in the case of overdose. Fresh foods offer safe sources of these vitamins, though too much liver can cause an oversupply of vitamin A. Consult your vet to help you determine if supplementation would improve your dog's health.

Always remember

- Dogs do better on two smaller meals a day than one big one. The dog does not get so desperately hungry with two meals and is in less danger of the sometimes fatal stomach torsion that happens when a big meal is consumed before exercise.
- Feed your dog in a quiet place and keep kids away from it while it is eating.
- Try to feed your dog at the same time every day.
- Serve food at room temperature.
- Keep the dog's dishes clean and the water supply fresh. This might take refreshing several times a day.
- Puppies need to eat more frequently than older dogs, but they are easier to house train if food is not available constantly.
- Food tidbits can be very helpful in training, but should be chosen for nutritional value and not used all of the time. Include the other kinds of praise, verbal and physical
- If there is a food (acceptable for human consumption) that you would like your dog to try, put it in your own mouth first, then offer it to the dog. Trainers sometimes put the bait they use to get dogs to perform at shows in their mouths.

CHAPTER NINE

The problem dog

Dog owners are sometimes confronted with confusing problems in their relationships with their dogs. A dog that once seemed to be so happy and well adjusted starts acting out in various ways. Our tendency is to gloss over problems in hopes that they will go away; inaction on the part of the owner can be seen as lack of leadership to the dog, who is looking to its person as leader. Passivity on the owner's part is taken for tacit consent or approval of the dog's new behavior.

DOG ATTACKS

Attacks by dogs are a very serious problem though often they are more the fault of the owner than the dog. Some attacks are brought on by aggressiveness (an attempt to dominate) and some happen because the dog is defending itself against a perceived threat (fear biters). Mail carriers and meter readers are common targets, since they have to enter dogs' territories.

Children are very susceptible to attack for several reasons. Their size makes some dogs think of them as inferior and easy to dominate. Their quick movements and squeaky voices bring out the hunting response in dogs. As well, children do not follow the recommended method of approaching a strange animal, which is to let the dog observe a while before slowly offering the dog a closed hand to sniff.

Children should be taught never to:

- Lunge at a dog or rush up to it
- Bother a dog while it is eating
- Hit or grab a dog

- Scream and run from a dog
- Bother a sleeping dog
- Tease any dog, especially one that is tied up

Though any dog can be a vicious biter, the most serious damage is usually done by larger, stronger dogs. The breeds considered by some insurance companies to be higher risk are the American Staffordshire Terrier, Boxer, Pit Bull, Chow Chow, Doberman Pinscher, German Shepherd Dog, Great Dane, Rottweiler and Siberian Husky. Some countries have gone so far as to ban specific breeds. Though people seem to be buying dogs for protection, there seem to many more stories of innocent people being harmed by dogs than of muggers and burglars being run off.

What can you do about the problem of dog attacks? When you choose a dog, consider very seriously choosing one of a breed known to be easygoing but trainable and establish a good relationship with it based on positive rewards, not harsh or violent training methods. Be consistent, so your dog does not receive mixed messages as to who is the boss and what behavior is acceptable. Never leave small children and babies alone with a dog. Always instruct older children in how to treat a dog. Facial contact with a dog should be discouraged since facial injuries are common, serious and disfiguring.

Times to be especially careful of dog bites

- When a dog has puppies to protect
- When a dog is hurt or in pain
- When a dog can no longer see well and might feel nervous and vulnerable
- When strange children are visiting
- When a delivery person comes to the door

Aggressive or defensive attacks causing bodily injury are probably the most serious problem facing dog owners. There are, however, many less serious but annoying problems that are the cause of dogs being abandoned or surrendered to shelters. The problems are almost always the fault of the humans involved and most can be solved with patient training.

SEPARATION ANXIETY

Some dogs become very agitated when left alone. They sometimes destroy things, break house training or bark incessantly when the owner is away. Vocalization is natural dog behavior designed to reunite the dog with its pack, but pet dogs can adapt to being left alone for reasonable periods of time. If the problem is mild, a distraction given to the dog when you leave can help. A hollow plastic toy packed with something like peanut butter can be a good diversion.

Your own attitude can make an enormous difference in how your dog sees separation. If you make a big fuss when you leave, your dog may become more anxious. If you are secure and matter-of-fact with the dog, it will have confidence in the safety of its surroundings and settle down better. Some dogs find a radio, playing the same music as when you are at home, to be reassuring. Some seem to like talk radio. Experiment to see what your dog likes.

Sometimes feeding your dog before you leave (with an opportunity to relieve himself) helps the dog sleep away the time you are gone. Another possible solution is to get another dog or a cat to keep your dog company. Let your dog have some quiet time to itself, when you are home, to lessen the disparity between your being there and being gone.

As part of your early training, you should desensitize your dog to separation by leaving for tiny periods of time (30 seconds), increasing the time very gradually. Some dogs might just need the security of the crate while the owner is away, although a full workday is usually too long for confinement. Having a neighbor or dogsitter pop in for a bit might be necessary. In most cases, a dog can learn to be alone with patient training.

JUMPING UP

Jumping up on people can be a very annoying dog habit. The dog is only trying to get close to your face to lick it in greeting and a show of submission, but jumping up can be painful or knock some people over. Some experts suggest stepping on the toes of the offending dog or kneeing her in the chest. Others suggest ignoring the dog and turning abruptly away. Putting out a flat hand in the dog's face, similar to the stay command is often effective, combined with the command "no."

CHEWING

Chewing is natural for puppies, but sometimes destructive chewing continues past puppyhood. The dog will not stop unless it is taught that such behavior is unacceptable. Take away the disallowed item with a stern "no" and substitute a chew toy. Take time to watch and correct the instant the dog goes for something inappropriate. Don't give old shoes to the dog to chew. Your dog will not be able to understand the difference between the one it can chew and the one it can't. Puppies must often be confined to areas where they cannot destroy belongings until they have learned the house rules. Really valuable things might need to go into storage until the problem has been solved.

DIGGING

Another natural dog activity is digging. Terriers especially love to dig, as it is what they were bred for. (Their name actually refers to dogs who "go to ground" to dig out small prey.) Dogs often dig to make a cool place to lie. Make sure your dog has a cool retreat in hot weather. Can you give him a cool place where it is acceptable to dig? Sometimes fencing off an area for the dog apart from precious gardens is a good solution. Digging can also be a means to escape, so make sure your fence goes right to the ground or is even dug in some if you have a digger. Digging can be recreational, so make sure your dog is getting some fun excursions. If you simply can't stand the digging, you can try startling the dog by putting some set mousetraps in the digging hole. They won't hurt the dog, but will give it some unpleasant associations with the hole. The same technique can discourage a dog from getting on the sofa or into the garbage if those are problems.

BARKING

A bit of barking when a stranger comes to the door should not be a problem if the dog responds to your command to be quiet after the initial bark. Don't pet and soothe the dog into silence, or you are rewarding behavior you want to reduce. Use the word "no" or "quiet" to silence the dog when you are home. Tell the dog to sit or lie down and make sure it does. Put the dog on a leash if you have trouble getting it to stop barking. A mild leash correction will give you more control. If the dog barks while you are away, try to discover what makes the dog bark and find a way to lessen the stimulus. The dog would probably prefer to spend the time you are gone in the house, since it is your family pack's den, in the dog's eyes. Play a radio to mask disturbing noises outside. You might have to pretend to leave, then give a stern vocal correction when the dog barks. You can also ask a friend to come to the door so you can practice your techniques.

THE SHY OR OVERLY SUBMISSIVE DOG

Shyness in dogs can be inherited or the condition can be the result of experience. The effect can be lessened with confidence-building interaction. Playing with the shy dog can help it become more outgoing. Entice your pup into interaction. Let it win the tug of war game. Early socialization can help a lot.

Let your dog see lots of people, men and women, adults and children, and advise the people to ignore the dog at first, then approach the dog gently. Some pups are obviously very submissive with littermates and are not usually the best bet for pets. These dogs need gentle handling since any harshness will cow them entirely. Submissive urination is not breaking of house training, but an attempt to express complete submission to you as leader. Don't scold your dog for this. Just clean it up without comment and work on building up the poor thing's self-confidence with lots of praise whenever it does something good.

VARIOUS PHOBIAS

Dogs sometimes have experiences that have frightened them and the fear of certain sounds or objects stays with them. Some dogs are afraid of riding in the car or of loud noises. You can help your dog become desensitized to such experiences by recreating the intimidating experience in a very mild way while at the same time giving the dog pleasant stimulation such as food. Quiet time in the car with the motor off and the doors open can lead eventually to a short ride. A favorite blanket or toy will ease the discomfort. A tape recording of, for instance, thunder can be played on very low volume while the dog is eating so it will associate the sound with a good experience.

THE DOMINEERING DOG

When a human does not take leadership of the family pack, the dog takes on the role. You will need to get leadership back. You will do this by controlling your dog's life. Here are some ways to do this:

- Have your dog drag its leash around the house for a while for quick corrections (no choke collar in this case).
- Control the dog's movement in the house by connecting it to various tie points in the house.
- Feed the dog only after making it wait while you eat (or pretend to eat).
- Give treats only after the dog has obeyed a command such as "sit."
- Give lots of exercise, but expect all commands to be obeyed during play.
- Make the dog sleep in his own bed and touch and move the bed now and then to establish your right to do so.
- Make the dog wait for you when going through a doorway.
- Praise submissive behavior. When the dog rolls on his back, give its tummy a scratch.

The leash dragging and dog tying are temporary measures until the dog gets the message. The rest are just standard procedure to keep your roles straight.

> Remember to make corrections at the time your dog is doing the "bad" thing. Don't yell or hit. Just speak with firm authority. Most dogs are quite comfortable doing what you demand.

CHAPTER TEN

Dog health

You can help your dog achieve its full potential for vitality through a program of health care that includes good nutrition, a safe and nurturing environment and regular veterinary care - plus a lot of attention and love from you. Regular veterinary care should have begun by the time you get your pup at around eight weeks of age. Older dogs from shelters will have been checked out by a vet and be up to date on all shots, though they might not have been cared for as well as is desirable. Preventative care is the best way to lessen the need for crisis care. The vet will be your partner in pet care. A yearly checkup at the time of vaccination should be the rule.

The general medical advice given in this book is not a substitute for a visit to a veterinarian. If you have concerns about your pet's health, always see a professional.

SPAYING AND NEUTERING

Spaying or neutering your dog can have many health benefits. Various diseases, such as mammary and testicular cancer, are drastically reduced through this procedure. Spaying relieves the owner of the problems associated with the female going into heat (accidental pregnancy, dribbling and staining, male dogs coming to call). Many behavior problems, such as wandering and aggressiveness, are reduced or eliminated by neutering. If you have a dog as a pet, it should - without a doubt - be neutered. If you wish to breed, you will need to learn a lot before you begin in order to be a competent breeder.

The millions of dogs that are put to sleep each year because there are more dogs than homes for them should convince any ethical person of the need to prevent many of the litters that are being born.

INOCULATIONS

Virtually every vet will advise you to have your pet inoculated against a number of serious canine diseases. Vaccinations offer a high degree of protection against diseases that have been killers for centuries and some more recent ones as well. Vaccines, which contain weakened forms of disease-causing agents (pathogens) protect by stimulating the dog's body to form antibodies specific to that agent. Since passive immunity is given to a puppy by its mother through her milk, and since those antibodies can interfere with the ones being newly formed, the pup will receive a series of injections from the age of about eight weeks to somewhere around 20 weeks in an attempt to balance the two kinds of immunity.

A number of vaccines are included in a full vaccination program. They will prevent the following diseases:

- **Canine distemper** A viral infection carried by wildlife that can affect a dog's nervous system.
- **Canine parvovirus** (CPV) Highly contagious viral infection, spread by fecal contamination, which can cause inflammation of the heart.
- **Hepatitis** Often fatal to young dogs, this disease can lead to chronic liver ailments.
- **Kennel cough complex** Causes inflammation of the voicebox and windpipe resulting in a hacking cough.
- **Rabies** Deadly disease affecting any warm-blooded animal, including humans. Yearly inoculation of companion animals is essential to keep immunity high. Puppies receive their rabies inoculations between three and six months and must be protected from contact with wildlife or unvaccinated animals until their rabies series is complete.

Inoculations work best on well animals, so the vet will examine your dog to make sure it is fit to receive the vaccine at the time of the visit and will reschedule the injections if necessary. Also, since there is some risk involved in vaccination, your vet will decide if some of the vaccines might not be necessary for your dog. For example, dogs not exposed to group dog situations such as kennels might not need kennel cough inoculation.

Some breeds have special problems with adverse reactions to immunization and others do not achieve high enough levels of immunity (called titres) with the normal number of shots. There are decisions to be made as to the best form of vaccine. Some vaccines, called fully attenuated vaccines, use killed disease organisms. Others, called modified live vaccines (MLV), use live organisms that have been disabled in some way so that actual disease does not occur from the inoculation. Because inoculation is a complicated subject with many decisions to be made, the best setting for the procedure is a private visit to the vet's office. While free clinics signify the government's deep concern for disease control, the complete care available at the vet's office will best serve your dog's health needs.

Dogs can have allergic reactions to inoculations. It is a good idea to have the shots early in the day and stay at the office for a while in case reactions occur. Signs of a bad reaction include depressed breathing, lethargy and greyish color of the gums.

THE HEALTHY DOG

Your dog, if healthy, will show signs of good health. He will move comfortably and will take an interest in his surroundings. He will have clean skin with no flakes, oiliness or odor. His coat will be shiny and evenly distributed, with no signs of fleas or other parasites. His eyes will be bright with no redness or discharge, not bulging or sunken. Healthy pink gums, neither pale nor too red, will meet tartar-free teeth evenly without receding. The anal region will be clean and dry with no inflammation. The feet will have trimmed nails and no damage to the pads. The insides of the ear will look clean and free of wax and odor (sometimes a sign of mites). Healthy dogs have spirit and energy, eat their regular diet without coaxing and follow a regular routine.

PARASITES

External parasites

Your vet will also be take measures to control parasites in your dog if they should occur. Dogs are host to many parasites, both internal and external. Even well-cared-for dogs can pick up parasites as they frequent places other dogs have been, such as parks and trails.

Persistent scratching can be a sign of skin parasites, the most common of which is the flea. A sign of flea infestation is tiny black specks, which are flea droppings, in your dog's fur and bedding. These droppings yield red stains when moistened on tissue paper, since they contain digested blood. A thorough vacuuming of the house and bathing of the dog are the first step to controlling the problem. Your vet might prescribe an insecticide and this should be used very carefully according to the vet's instructions.

Besides fleas, dogs can be afflicted with a variety of mites including sarcoptic mange mites which burrow into the skin and cause much itching; demodex mange mites that prefer hair follicles and cause little itching, but infection with pustules; harvest mites, also known as chiggers; and Cheyletiella mites, which cause flaking of skin and look somewhat like dandruff as they move through the dog's hair. Lice in dogs cause much irritation and lay their "nits" in the dog's hair. All of these pests can be controlled with special shampoos from your vet. Ticks attach themselves to a dog and enlarge as they feed on the dog's blood. Some carry the dangerous Lyme disease organism. Ticks should be swabbed with alcohol in order to loosen their grip. They should then be grasped with a tissue, as close to the skin as possible, and removed with a rotating motion.

Internal parasites

Your dog is also susceptible to internal parasites. Puppies are almost always infected by roundworms (ascarids) either in the womb or by way of their mother's milk. The hormones that occur in the female during pregnancy activate dormant worms encysted in her tissues and the larvae travel to the uterus and infect the pups. Then the pups pass eggs in their feces and the mother dog eats these (a tactic of many wild animal mothers to keep predators from finding their young) and is reinfected with the active form of the worm. Therefore, both mom and pups need deworming.

It is important to rid your dog of parasites for her own good and because the worms can be passed to other dogs and to humans as well. Worms affecting dogs include roundworms, tapeworms, hookworms and whipworms. Diagnosis is usually by way of microscopic examination of a fecal sample and treatment consists of prescribed medication. Some dogs need regular treatment because of their circumstances, while some dogs seem to stay clear of parasites without continued treatment.

Evidence of worms to look for in your dog would include egg sacs on the fur in the anal region, the dog licking and dragging its rear end, and actual worms in the feces. However, many dogs can have worms without symptoms and still pass them on to humans. The prudent course of action is to have your dog tested or treated periodically as advised by your vet. Your pet's wastes should be properly disposed of according to the laws of your community.

Heartworm, a serious threat to dog health, has been spreading northward over the years. These parasites, which can grow to a foot in length, are spread by a mosquito bite. An infected dog carries vast numbers of tiny larvae in its blood and these are passed from animal to animal when the mosquito feeds. After a developmental period of about two months, the heartworm moves to the heart where it matures. It causes heart damage sometimes leading to heart failure. Massive infestations can also damage liver and kidneys. The treatment for heartworm is hard on a dog, which must be kept from exercise during the treatment period, so preventative medicine is very much preferred. A dog must be tested and found to be free of heartworm before receiving the preventative treatment. Treatment may be very harmful to dogs that already have heartworm. The preventative medication is given for a period of time one to two months before mosquito season until a month past the end of mosquito season.

GENETIC DISEASES

Because of selective breeding practices, dogs suffer from a wide variety of genetic diseases. The most popular breeds seem to have more problems. This might be because there are more of them around to be studied, but the effect of indiscriminate and irresponsible breeders attempting to fill an increased demand might also have come into play.

Responsible breeders breed only from animals tested and found to be free of genetic disease, to the extent that this is possible. Some diseases have not been adequately defined or have no definitive diagnostic test. Some disorders, such as hip dysplasia, cannot be tested for adequately until the age of two years. Hip dysplasia is more common in larger dogs, though smaller breeds such as the American Cocker Spaniel, Miniature Poodle and the Shetland Sheepdog also suffer from it. The disease involves the malformation or disintegration of the ball and socket joint of the hips, leading to arthritis, pain and serious disability. Dysplasia is also a problem in dogs' elbows and a disorder called patellar subluxation affects the kneecap.

Genetic diseases affect almost all systems of the body. Inherited disorders of the eye include a group of problems such as progressive retinal atrophy (PRA) or degeneration (PRD) and the abnormal development that is called dysplasia. The age of onset of these conditions as well as the kinds of symptoms vary from breed to breed. Night blindness is sometimes an early sign. Diagnosis with an electroretinogram (ERG) can be made before the dog shows symptoms, so affected dogs can be removed from breeding programs. Collies often exhibit Collie eye anomaly and Shetland Sheepdogs are prone to corneal dystrophy (and should be checked for thyroid problems if they have the eye condition). Cataracts, glaucoma dry eye and other problems can also be inherited.

A tendency toward skin conditions such as seborrhea and dermatitis can be inherited. Such popular dogs as the Labrador Retriever and the Golden Retriever are susceptible to dermatitis. Inherited deafness is seen in such breeds as the Lhasa Apso and Miniature Poodle, the Rottweiler and the Dalmatian. Tiny dogs such as the Chihuahua, Pomeranian and Yorkshire terrier can suffer from collapsed windpipes. Inherited mouth problems include cleft palate, and abnormal dentition. Urinary diseases include kidney failure and bladder cancer. Examples of inherited nervous system disorders include epilepsy and behavior problems such as Springer Spaniel rage, an unexpected display of viciousness. Digestive conditions such as pancreatic hypoplasia and colitis are a problem for the German Shepherd Dog, and Boxers and Collies are fellow sufferers with colitis.

A disease called von Willebrand's disease affects many breeds including the American Cocker Spaniel, Dachshund, Fox Terrier, Golden and Labrador Retrievers, Poodles, Schnauzers, Yorkshire Terriers, Rottweilers and others. The disease is characterized by life-threatening bleeding brought on by a deficiency in a blood protein. Boxers and Dobermans are also susceptible to this condition as well as to serious heart conditions.

There are efforts being made to educate breeders and dog buyers on the part of such organizations as the Orthopedic Foundation for Animals (OFA) and the Institute for Genetic Disease Control in Animals (GDC) both of which encourage research into inherited canine diseases. The GDC makes available to interested parties, for a fee, the genetic records of individual dogs. This open registry helps track disease patterns and allows breeders to check the genetic makeup of bloodlines for better selection of mates. The Canine Eye Registration Foundation tracks inherited eye diseases, but does not make this information public. Unfortunately, there is as yet no easy formula that can guarantee the health of any given puppy.

DENTAL HEALTH

Your dog no longer has the diet of its wild ancestors, a diet that kept its teeth in good condition. The softer foods that dogs eat today do not provide the cleaning action that the natural diet gave and periodontal disease has become a serious problem. Though all dogs are susceptible, small breeds, with teeth crowded into smaller jaws, are especially prone to dental decay and gum problems. In periodontal disease, an accumulation of plaque on the teeth forms a hard scale that can cause the gum to pull away from the teeth. Food accumulates in the pockets that form, and resulting infections are a threat to the dog's overall health. Inflamed gums and bad breath are both signs of trouble. The remedy for advanced conditions is a thorough cleaning (called scaling) of the teeth to remove tartar and sometimes to clean out infected areas. A general anaesthetic is used during the procedure. Older dogs will have blood tests taken to make sure they can be safely anaesthetized. The chapter on grooming (chapter 7) suggests methods for tooth brushing to prevent these problems.

Five ways to keep your dog's mouth healthy

1. Brush your dog's teeth several times a week.
2. Select chew toys that are recommended for gum massage like Gumabone.
3. Have a dental check done once a year by the vet during the regular checkup.
4. Have done procedures that the vet recommends for dental problems.
5. Report to the vet any swelling, lumps or sores in the dog's mouth.

SIGNS OF TROUBLE

There are signs that should alert you to a health problem in your dog. You should make careful note of your observations and be able to report these to the vet to help make the diagnosis. Discharges of any sort from eyes, nose, ears or genitals merit attention. Drooling (aside from that of breeds that prone to regular drooling), inflamed gums, red or runny eyes, persistent scratching, hair loss, head shaking, limping or paralysis, coughing, diarrhea or constipation, bad breath, reluctance to be touched or handled, difficulty in urination, or dribbling, excessive change in weight or eating habits and lumps are all indications of something wrong with your dog. The symptoms should be discussed with your vet, since they could indicate serious illness. Lumps can turn out to be cysts, warts, abscesses or tumors. Some lumps should be tested (biopsy) to determine if they are cancerous. Early detection and treatment give a better chance for recovery from many conditions. A good time to check your dog for signs of illness is during grooming. You can run your fingers over the dog in a pleasant petting sort of way that you can both enjoy. If you begin this examination when the dog is a pup, it will become routine. If you begin with an older dog, begin gently and work up to a more thorough inspection.

THE VET'S EXAM

The vet's examination will cover the head (mouth, ears, eyes, etc.) and move on to listening to the heart and breathing, checking the temperature, feeling for swollen lymph nodes, checking the pulse, feeling the belly for swelling of the internal organs and checking the flexibility of the joints. The combination of this exam and your description of your dog's behavior, including any symptoms or complaints, should uncover most problems your dog might be having. Some conditions will require tests for diagnosis. Most medical tests available to people are also available for dogs. Your vet might find it necessary to refer your dog to a specialist, perhaps even one in another city.

Veterinary care can be expensive and some people find it reassuring to buy medical insurance to cover extraordinary expenses.

If medication is prescribed for an ailment, use it exactly as directed by the vet. Don't stop ahead of the prescribed schedule because the symptoms disappear. Don't use old medication because the condition looks like the one the medicine was prescribed for without checking with the vet. Sometimes symptoms look the same but the problem is different, and you could harm your dog.

FIRST AID

You should know something about first aid in case your dog or someone else's needs help sometime. It might be necessary to make a makeshift muzzle to keep an injured dog from biting. A strip of fabric, bandage or even a necktie can be used to tie around the dog's snout, then around the back of the neck. Be careful not to make it too tight and damage the throat or use it if there is already difficulty breathing. A blanket can be used to carry an injured dog.

Make a first-aid kit for your dog that contains:

- rectal thermometer (normal temperature for dogs is 39.5°C. or 101° and 102°F.)
- tweezers to remove bee and wasp stingers or ticks
- Kwik-Stop powder to stop bleeding nails
- antiseptic ointment
- penlight
- assorted bandages, pads and tape
- scissors
- cotton
- Pepto-Bismol
- buffered aspirin
- charcoal for poisoning (ask your vet about doses)
- hydrogen peroxide

In the case of suspected poisoning, induce vomiting if the dog is alert, the poisoning was within the hour and if you know that the swallowed substance was not corrosive (such as solvents). Hydrogen peroxide (by the tablespoon until the dog vomits) or salt water (one teaspoon to a cup of warm water) will cause vomiting. (Since salt can cause toxicity, use this method no more than once.) Never put anything down the throat of an unconscious dog. Ask your vet in advance about using activated charcoal to absorb poisons in cases that occur far from a vet. Take the suspected poison and a sample of the vomit and rush the dog to a vet. Wash poisons and paint off the fur with dog shampoo, but do not use any solvents or detergents. Have the phone number for the poison control center in your emergency phone list along with the vet's.

Wildlife encounters can lead to dog injuries. Porcupine quills should have their ends cut off, to cause them to shrink, before they are removed with pliers. Serious cases should go to the vet in case there are undetected quills in the mouth. Skunk odor is lessened by washing with tomato juice or mouthwash followed by a bath with dog shampoo. Wear gloves when you handle the dog in case the skunk was rabid and left saliva on the fur. Discuss the skunk encounter with a vet in case action is advised. Your dog should, of course, have an up-to-date rabies vaccination. In the case of a venomous snakebite, there will be two puncture wounds and the effects of the poison might include trembling, vomiting, drooling and collapsing. Apply ice to slow blood flow and take the dog to a vet.

Superficial wounds should be cleaned, an antiseptic ointment applied and then be bandaged loosely to prevent further injury. It might be necessary to clip away the fur near the injury. Serious falls and other accidents can cause internal bleeding and can be very serious.

If an injured dog is not breathing, you will need to resuscitate it by straightening the neck and blowing into the nostrils with your mouth over the end of the snout. The chest should rise if the air is getting into the lungs. If the dog's heart is not beating, you can attempt to start it with cardiac massage. Press with both palms on the chest behind the front legs as the dog lies on its side with the tongue hanging out. Give six pushes, then switch over to mouth-to-nose resuscitation for one blow, and alternate in that way until the heart starts beating. Then continue with resuscitation, checking the heart periodically. Get the dog to a vet as quickly as possible.

A dog that has almost drowned should be held by the back feet so the water can drain out. With a large dog, lay it on its side and lift the hind legs as high as you can. After 30 seconds of draining, give mouth-to-nose resuscitation until breathing begins, and take the dog to a vet.

Extremes of temperature can also cause serious injuries. Never leave a dog in a closed car in warm weather. The dog with heat stroke will be panting rapidly (a dog's only way of cooling itself since it cannot sweat) and might collapse. Cool it by immersing in cool, not cold water, and then drive to the vet with the car windows open for cooling.

Dogs can get hypothermia easily by swimming in cold water. Dry the dog and wrap in a warm blanket as you take it to the vet. The extremities, such as paws, ears and tail, are most at risk for frostbite and should be warmed gently in warm, not hot, water or warm cloths and gently massaged with a dry towel.

Small objects can become lodged in a dog's throat. You can use the Heimlich manoeuvre (sudden upward pressure under the ribcage causing air to be expelled forcefully through the mouth) on a dog, being careful, as with a child, not to be too rough. This should dislodge the object from the windpipe. Never allow your dog to play with small balls that can become stuck in the throat.

Such a tiny thing as a grass seed can lodge itself in a moist place in your dog's eye, nose or ear, genital openings or between the foot pads or toes. Check the feet frequently and watch for the dog sneezing a lot, chewing or licking some area or shaking its head.

SAFETY

Many of the injuries that require first aid can be prevented by some care on your part. Confine your dog to the safety of its own yard and use a leash when out for a walk. A safe yard is free from dangerous poisonous plants, water hazards, pesticides and electrical wires within reach. It also provides shelter from heat and cold as well as fresh water at all times.

Watch out for household poisons that could harm or kill your dog:

dishwasher granules	permanent markers	shoe polish
toilet-bowl cleaner	rat or mouse poison	floor wax
alcohol	sunscreen	nail-polish remover
bleach	paint	shoe polish
drain cleaner	hair dye	fabric softener
perfumes	non-safety matches	oven cleaner
mothballs	deodorants	Aspirin, Tylenol, Advil

A substance that kills in very small quantities and which dogs and cats find irresistible is **automobile antifreeze**. Watch your dog carefully in parking lots where antifreeze might have been spilled. A tablespoon is enough to kill your dog.

CHAPTER ELEVEN

Travelling with your dog

Travelling with your dog can be a royal pain or a real pleasure. Which it will be depends on how well-trained your dog is and how well you plan for the dog's presence and participation. There are lists of dog-friendly vacation spots and accommodations and even camps meant for people and their dogs. There will always be, however, places you cannot go accompanied by your dog and you will just have to accept that if you choose to travel with your pet. If you are not sure how your dog reacts to crowds and the kinds of places you will be visiting, take a few day trips first to test the waters. You might decide that your dog would be happier with a petsitter.

You will want to make sure your dog is well before starting out. All shots should be up to date and all health certificates should be carried with you. Keep them in the same travel folder you keep your own papers in. Inquire well ahead of time as to requirements for any places you will be visiting. Regulations can vary from state to state in the United States. Dogs should always wear identification. Travel ID should include your home address, the address you are going to or any stops along the way if possible. A good approach is to use disposable labels for temporary ID and put each day's motel or campsite address on the dog. The more permanent ID should include an emergency number (a relative or a friend back home), since you will not be answering your phone while you are travelling. Permanent identification by tattoo or injected chip is an excellent idea, but can be read by special means only. There is no substitute for ID tags on your dog.

CAR TRAVEL

Travelling in the car with your dog is very convenient since you can stop frequently for breaks and exercise. Your dog should be in the back seat, preferably attached to a seat belt with its own travel harness. That way, in case of an accident, the dog will be restrained and not end up flying around, landing on you. There are devices designed to connect the seat belt to the dog's collar, but a sudden stop could cause serious injury to the dog's neck. Dogs that are crate trained can travel in their crates if the car is big enough to hold it. Station wagons often can, but also can be fitted with grates that separate off the back section for the dog.

Dogs should not be allowed to stick their heads out of windows, even though they love it, because flying debris could harm their eyes. Nor should car windows be down enough for the dog to fall or jump out. It is totally unacceptable and irresponsible to put a dog in the back of a pickup truck. If it should be thrown out, it would surely be hurt or killed.

Dogs can be killed by the high temperatures in a closed car in warm weather. Only in cooler weather and with the windows open a crack can a dog be left in a car safely, and only for short periods of time. If you stop for a restaurant meal, try to park where you can see the car from the restaurant window. If you are delayed, go check on the dog. Don't leave the car doors unlocked. Dogs can be stolen.

The car travel kit

A car travel kit for your dog should include these things (many of the same items would be good to take when flying, too):

- your dog's normal food or a good travel substitute if you fix your own at home (try it before you leave)
- a can opener and a spoon, if your dog eats canned food
- food and water bowls
- a supply of home drinking water to use if the dog gets sick (or to clean the dog with)
- any medication your dog is on
- your regular dog shampoo – roadside parks have some nasty things to roll in
- plastic poo-pickup bags

- a sheet or blanket to cover your car seats and a clean one for the motel
- towels for that unexpectedly wet dog
- a 1.8 m (6 ft.) leash for regular use and an expanding leash for more freedom
- some "lost dog" posters with a picture of your dog just in case the unthinkable should happen
- dog toys

OVERNIGHTS

Some hotels and motels allow dogs and some do not. Travel guides (available through automobile associations) usually state which is the case for each establishment listed. Some hotels and motels allow pets that will be confined to their crates during the night. Dogs are not to be left alone in motel rooms unless they are crated. If your dog is a barker, it is not a good idea to leave it alone, even if crated. Ask for a room that allows easy access to the outside for your dog's bathroom trips.

Many campgrounds require dogs to be either on leash, in the car or in the tent. Keeping your dog on leash helps prevent unpleasant interactions between your dog and other campers or their dogs. Local dog lovers can sometimes advise you of safe places for a reliable dog to play off leash. Always, without exception, clean up after your dog.

AIR TRAVEL

Air travel can be very stressful for a dog and you must do everything possible to smooth the way. Dogs that are not healthy and dogs with pug noses are more at risk for air travel. The dog must be kenneled in an approved crate, big enough for the dog to stand in so the dog can brace itself in the event of turbulence. The non-leak bottom must be lined with absorbent material. Get your dog accustomed to its container well in advance. Label the crate with the words "live animal" and include arrows to show which way is up. Check the tags that are put on the crate to make sure they are correct.

Reserve early since animal space is limited, and make every effort to get a non-stop flight. If you have a stopover, make it long enough to retrieve the dog and give it a break with you. Be prepared for delays. Make sure your dog is boarded before you get on the plane. When you get off, tell the gate personnel that your dog is on board and ask that it be taken off the plane as soon as possible. If weather conditions are too hot or cold at either end of your trip, the dog will not be allowed to fly. Fly at night in hot weather and during the day in cold weather.

Much of the worry about flying with your dog is having him out of your sight. Very small dogs can travel with you in the airplane cabin if confined to a carrier small enough to fit under the seat in front of you. Special bags with screened ventilating sides are available. You are allowed to reach into the bag to comfort your dog, but he must be inside the bag from the time you enter one terminal until you exit the one at the end of your flight.

THE NON-TRAVELING DOG WHEN YOU TRAVEL

What can you do if you just can't take your dog on a trip? You have several options. A good dog-loving friend with a dog of her own to take in your dog is a wonderful option. Perhaps you can trade off dogsitting; both dogs will enjoy it. Some vets board dogs, as do some breeders. Some people have good luck with arranging for a housesitter to live in and care for everything. You have to be able to trust this person entirely. Ask friends for recommendations for good kennels if that is the route you might wish to take.

You'll want to inspect the facilities and ask a lot of questions before leaving your dog in a place you do not know well. Even if you plan to take your dog with you, it is a good idea to have a plan in mind in case there are last-minute problems with your own travel and the dog has to stay home. Emergency travel on your part might also make arrangements necessary on very short notice. Your own vet might be able to give you good advice on such matters.

CHAPTER TWELVE

Caring for the older dog

Whether you have had your dog since puppyhood or adopted a grown dog, you will want to make your dog's senior years as pleasant as possible. Your dog's sense of well-being and joy of living come from simple things such as good food, a warm bed, kind people, appropriate play and freedom from pain. These are things you can provide.

How do you know when your dog can be classified as "geriatric," or older? As with people, dogs age at different rates. In general, the smaller breeds of dogs live longer than the larger breeds, with smaller breeds averaging a life span of 12 or more years, medium-sized about 10 years, large about nine and the giant breeds living, on the average, seven. Dogs are considered to be geriatric when they have lived three-quarters of their expected life span.

Signs of aging in your older dog might include impaired eyesight or hearing, changes in the skin or coat, changes in bowel habits, mouth problems including teeth and breath and difficulty with movement. Weight gain is also common in older dogs and brings with it a number of health problems.

DIAGNOSIS AND TREATMENT

Advances in veterinary medicine have made it possible to treat many of the problems that have been associated with old age. As is the case with our own health, spotting problems early is important. A special geriatric screening around the age of seven is a good idea. Your veterinarian has tests that will show problems in areas such as heart, lung, liver and kidney function so that these can be treated before they progress. Most treatments available to humans are also available for dogs through a veterinarian.

The diseases that afflict older dogs will sound familiar, since many are the same that affect humans. Heart problems include heart murmur, indicating degeneration of heart valves, leakage and congestive heart failure. Small dogs are particularly susceptible to such problems. Fortunately, there are medications to control some of these conditions.

Bone and joint disease

All dogs, but especially older dogs, are susceptible to various types of bone and joint problems. These problems may be divided into the non-inflammatory and inflammatory types. The non-inflammatory joint diseases include degenerative joint disease (osteoarthritis and osteoarthrosis), osteochondrosis, which includes hip dysplasia, and other conditions. The inflammatory joint diseases (arthritis) include the blood-borne conditions caused by infectious wounds as well as non-infectious or immunologic conditions such as rheumatoid arthritis.

The physical symptoms of these conditions include distention of joints, reduced range of motion, joint misalignment, erosion of cartilage and the underlying bone, as well as pain, stiffness and muscle atrophy. The causes of these joint and bone diseases vary, but include, in some cases, a genetic (breed) predisposition. Since some of these same symptoms can also indicate other serious diseases, including bone cancer, a vet's diagnosis is needed. Your vet can rule out causes of pain such as the anterior cruciate ligament rupture (ACLR) and luxating patellas which occur mostly in some of the smaller dogs under 11.3 kg (25 lb.) but are also seen in larger breeds.

Treatments for degenerative joint disease and related conditions might include restriction of activity, drug therapy, weight reduction to reduce strain on the joints and even replacement of a diseased joint. Drugs that are sometimes used include non-steroidal anti-inflammatory drugs (NSAIDs), which include various painkillers and which can have serious side effects, the most common being stomach ulcers and renal failure. Also used are the corticosteroids that can have a negative effect on the cartilage if used in too high doses or for too long. These drugs are used mostly for short-term treatment of acute conditions.

Other recent treatments include alternative therapies such as nutritional supplements, acupuncture, herbal treatments and homeopathy. Orally administered nutritional supplements such as glucosamine (from the exoskeletons of molluscs or from cartilage) and chondroitin sulfate (obtained from shark cartilage or bovine sources) may help in the repair of damaged hyaline cartilage in joints. Consult your vet about supplementing your old dog's diet with added vitamin C, glucosamine and fatty acids contained in evening primrose and fish oil. Some nutritional supplements are formulated to include antioxidant vitamins, trace elements and fatty acids, such as omega 6, omega 3 and monosaturates, that are thought to benefit dogs with joint problems.

Acupuncture can be used to stimulate circulation and the release of endorphins, the natural painkillers within the body. Such treatment must be administered by a practitioner licensed by the International Veterinary Acupuncture Society.

You can contribute to the relief of your dog's joint discomfort with mild exercise. Swimming is excellent for this purpose. More frequent and less taxing exercise can help keep joints moving freely and enhance general well-being.

How old is old?

While folk wisdom says that one human year equals seven dog years, this formula can be misleading. A more accurate comparison looks like this:

Dog age	Human age
8 months	13 years
2 years	24 years
3 years	28 years
5 years	32 years
7 years	38 years

From this point on, multiply dog age by 5.

Cancer

Cancer can occur in animals of all ages, but age is a strong factor since the changes that can lead to cancer sometimes take awhile to accumulate. There are differences in susceptibility in dogs according to size, breed and even skin pigment. Cancers of the mammary glands and testicles are common in dogs that have not been neutered. Females have their risk reduced radically when spaying occurs before the first estrus, or period of heat. Males affected by a condition called cryptorchidism (undescended testicles), have a much higher chance of developing cancer of this organ. Neutering greatly reduces the odds of your male dog developing testicular cancer as well as several diseases of the prostate. Your neutered female dog has less chance of developing mammary cancer as well as a serious type of uterine infection. For these reasons, neutering is one of the best examples of preventative treatment you can give your dog.

When grooming your older dog, or even just petting him, run your hands over his body checking for lumps, bumps and growths. Some are harmless, such as benign fatty tumors, but some, such as the mast cell tumor, can be life-threatening, and all should be brought to the attention of the vet.

Weight gain

Weight gain is a serious problem in aging dogs. Though some dogs can be given free access to their food all day, most dogs cannot be trusted not to overeat, so it is up to you to control your dog's caloric intake. The various grades of commercially produced dog foods are discussed in the nutrition chapter and generally the same rules apply for the aging dog as for the younger. Some dog-food manufacturers produce a food that is specially formulated for the less active, older dog. There are products with lower caloric levels for chubby dogs and also products with a higher caloric content for dogs that become thin as they age. Some of the geriatric formulations contain higher levels of vitamins C, E and the associated beta-carotene for their antioxidant qualities.

While it was once thought that higher levels of protein put a strain on the kidneys of older dogs, this has been shown not to be true. On the question of protein intake, you should consult your vet, since he can take into consideration every aspect of your dog's current health status. There are some conditions that would be best treated with a specialized, even prescription, diet.

Weight gain itself can have different causes. Older dogs tend to be less active, so fewer calories are burned. It might be necessary to reduce somewhat the actual amount your dog eats. Some breeds, such as Labrador Retrievers, Dachshunds, Basset Hounds, Golden Retrievers and Beagles, seem to have a genetic predisposition to obesity. There are also hormonal imbalances having to do with thyroid and pituitary function that can cause weight gain.

Incontinence

The old dog that begins suddenly to urinate in the house often has a health problem. Bladder infections and loss of muscle tone are both treatable with drugs. Hormone-responsive incontinence is effectively treated with estrogen for females and testosterone for males. A non-hormonal drug called phenylpropanolamine can also help by restoring the constricting function of the urethral sphincter. Still, some leakage might be unavoidable. If the main time for leakage is at night, take your dog out last thing before you go to bed, encourage your dog to sleep in his bed and line the bed with towels that you launder frequently. Do not scold your dog, who often feels embarrassed already.

Dental care

Another area of health that is of great importance with all dogs, but especially older dogs, is dental hygiene. Prevention is usually easier than treatment. Brushing your dog's teeth will help remove food particles and prevent the buildup of tartar, or scale. If tartar has developed, it will probably be necessary for the vet to remove the buildup. General anaesthetic is the rule for such a procedure unless the dog is unusually co-operative and the buildup is very light.

You will also want to watch for danger signs having to do with your dog's mouth, such as pawing at that region, blood in the saliva, growths on the gums, excess salivation or difficulty swallowing. Anything of this sort calls for prompt medical attention. Your vet will also check for evidence of periodontal disease –

including problems with the gums and the bone holding the teeth in place.

Aside from the problems of tartar accumulation, there is also the wear and tear brought on by years of chewing. Attrition is the normal tooth-to-tooth wear that cannot be helped. Abrasion is the damage done when the dog chews on something inappropriate such as rocks. You should discourage you dog from such practices if possible and substitute suitable chew toys.

Anaesthesia

The question of safety of anaesthesia for the elderly dog comes up over and over. Anaesthesia always carries some risk, even with healthy patients. When the proper tests are carried out before anaesthesia, the risks are greatly reduced. Laboratory tests provide a profile of your dog's overall health and ability to undergo anaesthesia successfully. Fluids by intravenous drip and pre-op and post-op antibiotics for dental procedures give added insurance of a good outcome. You are very important to your dog's health at this time because you must follow the vet's instructions to the letter. An empty stomach is absolutely necessary during anaesthesia so that your dog does not suffer from inhalation of stomach contents and die.

> You must provide care as instructed when your pet comes home, especially if the sedation has not worn off completely. Some throat irritation is to be expected from the breathing tube that was used to deliver the anaesthetic and your dog might have a cough for a while. You should be watching for any unusual behavior on the part of your dog and advise the vet of it.

Eyes and ears

The old dog's eyes may gain a bluish-grey tint over the years. This condition, called lenticular sclerosis or nuclear sclerosis, is the result of compression of fibers in the lens as well as loss of moisture, which causes the lens to become denser over the years. It does not usually affect vision to any great degree. No treatment is needed.

Some dogs develop cataracts, characterized by a true clouding of the lens. Some cataracts are incomplete and do not cause serious blindness. Others are serious enough to need surgical removal that should be done by a veterinary ophthalmologist.

Cataracts can have an hereditary basis. Many popular breeds have a high incidence of hereditary cataracts. The list includes Standard, Miniature and Toy Poodles, Golden Retrievers, German Shepherd Dogs, Chow Chows, Siberian Huskies, West Highland Terriers, Beagles, American Cocker Spaniels, Boston Terriers, Labrador Retrievers, Miniature Schnauzers, Old English Sheepdogs, Staffordshire Bull Terriers and Chesapeake Bay Retrievers. To a lesser degree, cataracts can be the result of diabetes mellitus, injury to the eye, ocular inflammation or inherited retinal diseases.

Older dogs' fading eyesight is less upsetting to them and their enjoyment of life than we might expect. They seem to be able to get around moderately well in familiar surroundings. The same goes for reduced hearing. If you are aware of your dog's disabilities, you can make provisions for them. The dog's environment must protect him from dangers he will not see or hear coming. Keep him on a leash outside the fenced yard.

MAKING YOUR OLDER DOG COMFORTABLE

There are some things you can provide that will make life much easier for the older dog. A soft bed, low to the floor, in a warm location free of drafts will be appreciated. If couch-sitting is allowed, but the jump is too high now, some kind of booster would be a good idea. A sweater on a cold day, especially for short-haired dogs, is beneficial, as is a doggy life-jacket for the oldster who still likes to swim, but is not as strong as he once was. Some people use raised feeding dishes. If you have a younger dog as well, make sure the oldster does not have to compete for his share of food at mealtimes. Don't make the senior dog put up with too much pestering from a playful younger pet. Special equipment can help disabled dogs. There are even strap-in carts for dogs that no longer have full use of their hindquarters.

EUTHANASIA

When the quality of your dog's life has declined to a certain point, you might decide to have him put to sleep. The process, called euthanasia, consists of the painless injection of an overdose of anaesthesia. Medical advances have made it possible to treat diseases that were once thought to be untreatable, but sooner or later, every dog wears out. You might want to spare you pet unnecessary suffering. The decision will no doubt be a very hard one, but you need to have your dog's best interests at heart. Your vet can discuss the matter with you and give you information that might help you know when to say goodbye.

CHAPTER THIRTEEN

Having fun with your dog

Your well-trained and well-loved dog is going to be a pleasure for you much of the time. The companionship you get from your dog will be rewarding and worth all of the time and attention you give your pet. Some dogs, such as ranch dogs and police dogs, naturally spend hours working with people. Others find the hours that their owners are away working long and lonely. Sometimes it a good idea for you to schedule some funtime with your dog. It will be good for both of you.

There are the organized activities under the auspices of dog clubs and organizations, and fun stuff you can do, on your own, around the house or on an outing.

EVENTS SPONSORED BY KENNEL CLUBS AND OTHER GROUPS

If you find you are interested in showing your dog, you will need to join a local breed group to help you learn the ropes, and there is a lot to learn. The club will also give you and your dog the companionship of the other dog owners and their dogs. (Directories of breed clubs appear in each edition of *Dogs in Canada Annual* and may also be found on the Web under each breed name.) Maybe you don't want to show, but want to learn more about dogs in general or your breed. Some clubs specialize in one breed and others are all-breed clubs.

A good place to start learning about dog shows is at the match where everybody is practicing. The dogs are learning and the judges are learning. No points are given. Dress is casual and there are lots of opportunities to talk to dog people.

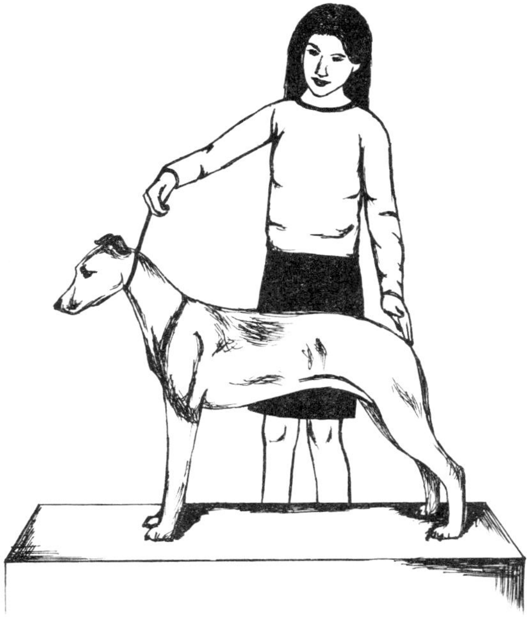

Obedience trials are a very popular activity. Dogs and handlers do the regular sit-stay-down-retrieve drills. Utility trials have the dogs performing very exacting exercises such as responding to signals only, without spoken command; finding articles with the master's scent; and retrieving the article indicated by the master. These exercises demonstrate real teamwork.

Field trials test dogs for the skills their breeds are known for and are held in the field. Dog owners work hard to train their dogs to bring out their natural talents. Some owners work for points and prizes and others for the pure enjoyment of working with the dog. As with obedience trials, there are trials for points, but also sanctioned trials that are just for practice or fun. Field trials include trials for the trailing hounds that include the Beagle, the Basset Hound and the Dachshund. There are also separate specialized events for Pointers, Retrievers, Spaniels, Coonhounds and Terriers. The graceful sighthounds, also called gazehounds, are tested in the lure coursing event in which they race after a mock prey being dragged through a course.

There are many other types of events sponsored by the dog clubs. There are tracking tests involving following a scent trail that has been laid down for the purpose. There are also more advanced tests that include discrimination and some that have time limits. In tracking tests, individual dogs either pass or fail, rather than compete against each other for placement. Dogs whose breeds were developed to pull carts (Bernese Mountain Dog, Saint Bernard, Rottweiler, Collie, Bouvier des Flandres and Newfound-land) have an event to test the various aspects of this skill. The Newfoundland is also involved in tests for water rescue. Weight-pulling contests are also held and have their own specific association to set rules and standards. Dogs are divided into categories by weight and pull a loaded sled a prescribed distance. Terriers are tested for their digging skills in events held by the American Working Terrier Association. They can earn Junior, Senior or Master Earthdog credentials. The World Wide Web can put you in touch with people who enjoy these activities and can help you get into them.

Many races of different lengths test the prowess of the sled dog breeds. The International Sled Dog Racing Association, with worldwide membership, holds events that are often sponsored by corporations that give cash prizes. Included are the short sprint races, the load-hauling freight races and long-distance races. There are even gig races in which the dogs pull a three-wheeled cart on earth rather than snow. Participants include the typical northern breeds such as the Alaskan Husky and the Malamute, as well as many other breeds.

Herding breeds are tested with a variety of trials involving herding various kinds of animals. There are many titles given by many different organizations including the Australian Shepherd Club of American and several Border Collie groups. Skills tested include gathering, driving, penning and doing it all with the proper style. There is a certification program for herding breeds to attest to the presence of inborn ability without training.

Schutzhund trials (schutzhund being the German word for guard dog) test for tracking, obedience and protection, and the title has three levels. Breeds most often involved are German Shepherd Dogs, Rottweilers and Doberman Pinschers though many other breeds take part. This sport has its own organization and magazine. The tests are very exacting and training is rigorous. In the protection portion of the trials, the dog attacks a person posing as an attacker.

Agility is a new sport that can be fun for dog and owner alike. Dogs run courses made up of at least 10 obstacles (which must be approved as safe by the United States Dog Agility Association). Obstacles include jumps of various types, weave poles, teeter-totter, open and closed tunnels, suspended hoop and the A-frame climb.

A dog sport that spectators love and dogs seem to relish is flyball. Dogs work in teams and run relays. Each dog in turn jumps four low hurdles on its way to the ball-release box. Hitting the box with a paw, the dog releases the ball, catches it and returns to the start so the next dog on the team can repeat the process. You'll need to join a group, of course, to be on a team. Flyball is a highly organized dog sport with numerous clubs and governed by the North American Flyball Association in Illinois. There is a British association, as well. There are also organized flying-disc competitions such as the Flying Disc Dog Open, in which highly talented dogs and owners strut their acrobatic talents.

A good place to find out what is going on in your neighborhood is the World Wide Web. Such sites as that of *Dog World Magazine* (www.dogworldmag.com) present calendars of events for various kennel clubs.

TEACHING YOUR DOG TRICKS

Sometimes it can be fun to show your dog off with a few tricks. Some dogs take to tricks very easily. Shaking hands is taught with the dog sitting down. Tap the back side of the forearm and give the command "shake." When your dog lifts his paw, take it in your hand and praise him.

Jumping into your arms is an impressive trick if you are big enough to catch and hold your dog. Squat down, give the command you have chosen for the trick and, with vocal encouragement, have your dog crawl onto your lap. Praise him lavishly. Then, see if your dog will jump onto your knees as you catch him in your arms. When that step is accomplished, you can start squatting down not so far, on the way to standing fully upright while your dog jumps into your arms.

Dogs can be taught to jump hurdles. Start with a low solid fence or other objects. Step over it yourself and then encourage your dog, on leash, to jump over it. Then you can run up to the hurdle and have your dog jump over it, still on leash. Try it without the leash. Keep the height reasonable for the size and condition of your dog, and don't try it until your dog is over a year old, since bones are not adequately developed until then. When having the dog attempt jumps on outings, be very careful to avoid any kind of dangerous fences, such as barbed wire or stakes. Low fallen logs make great jumps. You can fashion a hoop out of garden hose and have your pooch jump through that. Use a different command for hoop jumping just to keep things straight.

Teaching a dog to "speak" or bark on command is accomplished by getting the dog to bark, saying the command to make the association, then praising the dog. You will have to experiment with what brings on a bark with your particular dog.

Some people enjoy singing with their dogs. If your dog ever howls at sirens, you have a "singer" and can get a good songfest going by making the same low howling note as your dog, then expanding the howl to other notes and adding syllables such as row, row, rah, row. Incidentally, you will also want to practice turning off the howl.

WATER ACTIVITIES

Some dogs are natural swimmers, but some need to be introduced gently and encouraged to swim. A lake with a very gradual incline is excellent. You can go in with your dog and entice it out with treats or toys, or just with your voice. You can also throw something to fetch if your dog likes to go after things, but be careful not to throw things too far, since any difficulties or bad experiences your dog has can make it much less likely to want to go in the water again. Be very careful with rivers and currents or water that is too cold. On winter walks, don't let your dog go onto the ice unless it is thick enough for you to go on safely, too.

Many dogs adore boats. Train your dog to remain still in a boat, especially a canoe. You can get a lifejacket for your dog at the pet store or by catalogue. When riding in a motorboat, hold your dog as the boat approaches the dock, since dogs will sometimes try to jump out, misjudge the distance and be hurt.

DOGS AND KIDS

The 4H organization, in both Canada and the United States, has projects in which kids learn about dogs and how to be good dog handlers. The 4H club members give speeches and demonstrations, conduct dog-training workshops and have fundraisers at which they wash dogs and sell homemade dog treats and toys. The 4H Fairs allow the kids to show their dogs, make new friends and learn to be judges. As well, 4Hers take part in many worthwhile activities: dog therapy, working as volunteers in small animal clinics and humane societies and raising guide dogs for the blind. The national kennel clubs also have show divisions especially for young people. Older kids who are comfortable with dogs can help out by walking dogs of people who are not able to do so themselves.

DOG THERAPY

If your dog is calm and even-tempered, you might want to take part in a pet therapy program. Therapy dogs visit people in hospitals and retirement homes and make a wonderful contribution to the lives of the people there. Special pet-therapy courses will prepare you and your dog for the situations you will encounter.

PLAIN AND EASY FUN

There are some wonderful activities you can do with your dog without a great deal of planning, organization or joining a group. Some of the things you might have enjoyed doing on your own can be even more fun with your dog. Outings broaden your dog's life, alleviating the boredom that can come from staying at home a lot. As well, play is extremely important in the bonding that goes on between a dog and its owner.

Walking can be very relaxing. A nature walk, with time to watch frogs by a stream or wade in the shallow water, is a dog's idea of paradise. Your dog will be able to tell what crossed a path yesterday or the week before. A neighborhood walk, on leash, can be your dog's catalog of familiar scents. Your dog already knows the neighborhood from the thousand smells she has picked up. Let the dog see what it has been smelling. Meeting people and dogs on walks is part of an ongoing socialization program that should have started when the dog was a pup.

Jogging, or brisk walking if that works better for you, can have healthful benefits for you and your dog. You will first want to train your dog to heel and encourage him to run at your side, far enough forward for you to keep track of him. If you give your dog time to fool around dog-style before starting the jog, he will not be so crazy to stop for every scented bush. You might still be nice enough to stop now and then so your dog can sniff. Keep your dog on a leash unless you are sure he will stay right with you and you are well away from all car traffic. Cars and dogs just don't mix. Hot weather, especially if it is also humid, can put your dog at risk for heat stroke if you ask him to go too far, or too fast. Even in cooler weather, you must work up to the longer distances gradually. Watch for things on the path that could hurt your dog's feet.

Check his pads frequently for damage and keep his toenails the proper length. Hot asphalt can burn your dog's feet.

A really enjoyable thing to do with your dog is having your dog pull you on cross-country skis. The sport is called skijoring and does require some equipment, such as a harness for your dog, lead lines and a belt for yourself. A standard sled-dog training harness will do fine and can be ordered from supply houses. There should also be a release for the line. The pooch needs to be in good shape and weigh at least 13.6 kg (30 lb.), though 18.1 kg (40 lb.) is probably better. Two dogs can pull together, as they do on dog sleds. Some people join clubs to do skijoring, or go to special resorts (some even supply trained dogs) that welcome your dog, but you can have lots of fun on hiking trails. Skiers can be annoyed if you mess up groomed trails, so look for some that are not groomed. Watch out for horses and snowmobiles. Although it might seem a drag to stop, you should always clean up after your dog. (No snow? Some athletic folks manage to have their dogs pull them on rollerblades.)

A good game of fetch is a wonderful way to motivate your dog to exercise when you might not want to exert yourself too much or time is too short for a walk. You can throw a ball or toy, a stick or a plastic flying disc. Many dogs will bring it back to you without prompting because they want you to throw it again. You might have to encourage some dogs, by using the recall command, but the sportier dogs will want to go on long past the time when your arm is worn out. Be careful not to throw the object where the dog might run into something dangerous like traffic.

Dogs bred for certain uses tend to like play that recreates the situations for which they were bred. Some kinds of dogs, particularly some herding breeds, might prefer other kinds of games, thinking fetch to be somewhat pointless. Some herders like to chase and be chased. They might bring you the ball, but want you to chase them to get it back. This is not always the case, however, Australian Shepherds being some of the best flying-disc retrievers around. Some large dogs like to capture and hold a toy. A deflated ball works well. Hide and seek is a marvelous game to play with your dog. Throw a ball and, while the dog is going to retrieve it, hide and let your dog find you. You can also hide one of his toys and tell the dog to "go find." Show the dog the toy first and give the stay command while you hide it.

Some dogs just love water, even if they are not water dogs. Get a rigid plastic pool for your pooch. Fill it up and watch your dog have a great time. Toss the ball into the water for your dog to fetch. This is cool fun on a hot day.

Many experts warn not to play tug with your dog because the game is a dominance game for dogs. With certain precautions, you should be able to enjoy a game of tug. Don't pull too hard or jerk because you might harm your dog's teeth. Be sure to be the one who finishes with the item and then puts it away. You are the boss and you control the item. However, if you have a timid, submissive dog whose ego really needs bolstering, you can let the pooch win some of the time.

APPENDIX ONE

Dog trivia

1. **Up close and personal** Dogs in history have sometimes been man's intimate companions. Mexican hairless dogs and the lovely speckled Peruvian Inca Orchid served as bedwarmers, while the tiny Pekinese were carried around in the sleeves of Chinese courtiers.

2. **Don't tell Rin Tin Tin** Police in Germany say the German Shepherd Dog has lost its crime-fighting edge. They are replacing it with the burly French herding dog, the Beauceron.

3. **Canine cross-dresser** The numerous dogs that have played the lovely Collie Lassie in movies and on TV were not lassies at all, but were really males. The first Lassie, in the movie *Lassie, Come Home*, was played by Pal, a male Collie who had been hired to play the stunt-double for the female star. Pal did such an amazing job fording a raging river and playing dead that he got the part regardless of his gender. Pal's trainer, Rudd Weatherwax, and his family, have continued to raise subsequent Lassies, up to Lassie VIII, a distant grandson of Pal.

4. **Guide dogs** Many ancient cultures sacrificed dogs on graves or buried them with the dead in hopes the dogs could serve as guides through the underworld. In China, this practice was eventually replaced by the use of clay dog figurines, complete with molded on leading harnesses.

5. **The Doberman Pinscher** was the official combat dog of the U.S. Marines in World War II. A memorial statue honoring Kurt and other 24 other Doberman wardogs was dedicated in July 1998 at the College of Veterinary Medicine at the University of Tennessee.

6. **Dog extremes** While the short-legged Pekinese walks at a snail's pace, the long-legged greyhound can reach a speed of 66 km/h (41 miles/h). The Chihuahua stands just 15-23 cm (6-9 in.) at the shoulder, a true shrimp compared to the Great Dane or the Irish Wolfhound, whose shoulders can reach 81-90 cm (32-35 in.) .

7. **Doggie invitation** What does it mean when your dog bows down to you with its rump in the air? He is asking you to play.

8. **What a schnoz!** The average dog possesses 200 million scent receptors compared to just five million in humans. But humans have six times as many taste buds. What about hearing? A dog can locate sounds very quickly and can hear sounds four times further away than we can. No wonder they don't like thunder.

9. **Pups in a hurry** The gestation time for dogs is just 63 days.

APPENDIX TWO

Other information sources

BOOKS

The Encyclopedia of the Dog, by Bruce Fogle, Firefly, 1995.

The Dog's Mind, by Bruce Fogle, Pelham Books, 1992.

The Complete Dog Book: A Comprehensive, Practical Care and Training Manual and a Definitive Encyclopedia of World Breeds, by Peter Larkin, Mike Stockman and John Daniels, Acropolis, 1997.

Living with Dogs, by Henry and Mary Ellen Korman, Raincoast, 1997.

American Kennel Club Dog Care and Training, by American Kennel Club, Howell Book House, 1991.

201 Ways to Enjoy Your Dog: A Complete Guide to Organized U.S. and Canadian Activities for Dog Lovers, by Ellie Milon, Alpine Publications, 1990.

Your Healthy Pet, by Any Marder, Rodale Press, 1994.

Your Purebred Puppy: A Buyers Guide, by Michelle Lowell, Henry Holt, 1990.

Raising Rover, by Judith Halliburton, St. Martin's Press, 1996.

Choosing and Caring for a Shelter Dog, by Bob Christiansen, Canine Learning Center Publishing Division, 1996.

Second-Hand Dog: How to Turn Yours into a First Rate Pet, by Carol Lea Benjamin, Howell Book House, 1988.

The Canadian Dog Owner's Companion: A Guide to Selecting, Caring for and Training Your New Dog or Puppy, by Donna Davidson and Penny Manning, Macmillan Canada, 1997.

MAGAZINES

Dog Fancy, Fancy Publications, Irvine, CA.

Dogs in Canada, Apex Publishing, Etobicoke, ON (by the month and annual)

Dog World, PJS Publications, Peoria IL.

WEBSITES

www.dogworldmag.com	Official website of *Dog World* Magazine
www.dogs-in-canada.com	Official website of *Dogs in Canada* Magazine
www.k9web.com/dog-faqs/lists/faq-list.html	Extensive list of websites by Cindy Tittle Moore
http://dogs.miningco.com/	Another incredible list of links of dog-related web sites
www.netpets.org/dogs/dogresc/doggrp.html	Directory of dog rescue groups
www.the-kennel-club.org.uk	Official site of the United Kingdom Kennel Club
www.akc.org	Official site of the American Kennel Club
www.ckc.ca	Official site of the Canadian Kennel Club
www.ukcdogs.com	Official site of the United Kennel Club
www.ckcusa.com	Official site of the Continental Kennel Club
http://netvet.wustl.edu/	A veterinary resources website
www.canismajor.com/dog/guide.html	Dog Owner's Guide
www.canismajor.com/dog/inetg.html	Dog Owner's Guide to the Internet
www.dog-play.com	listing dog related recreation